The Write Mentoring

The essential handbook for emerging and established writers

Published by New Writing North, 2007

New Writing North
Culture Lab
Grand Assembly Rooms
Newcastle University
King's Walk
Newcastle
NE1 7RU

New Writing North Limited 3166037
Registered charity number 1062729

Editors: Claire Malcolm and Rachael Ogden
Publications manager: John Adair
Cover design: Tommy Anderson at Baseline Shift
Printed by Cromwell Press

New Writing North acknowledges the financial support it receives from the Cultural
Sector Development Initiative at Arts Council England, North East.

ISBN 978-0-9552423-4-2

Celebrating
10 years of
New Writing North
1996–2006

ARTS COUNCIL ENGLAND

Project Part-Financed
by the European Union

European Regional
Development Fund

Foreword

I have run mentoring schemes for professional writers for New Writing North since 1998. We began working in this way as a creative response to the professional development needs that the emerging writers who we were working with presented to us. Mentoring appealed instinctively to me as it closely mimics the productive creative relationships that I have seen many writers have with each other.

Over the years I have set up mentoring schemes for poets, novelists and scriptwriters. It started in a very informal way and then, when I began to see the fantastic results that mentoring brought, moved towards creating a structure for the schemes.

Now, as a wider understanding of the term mentoring has developed within the creative writing world, I am asked regularly to advise on schemes or to share our good practice with others. This book encompasses everything that New Writing North knows about mentoring, along with much other useful and interesting material and points of view gathered by authors Sara Maitland and Martin Goodman.

Sara and I have worked together on mentoring programmes for a number of years and over this time we have discussed how the schemes work and how things could be further developed. I have learnt a great amount from working with her as well as from other regular New Writing North mentors such as scriptwriter Steve Chambers and poet Linda France. I'd like to take this opportunity to thank everyone who has participated in our schemes over the years and helped to define and refine the learning.

Our hope is that this book will help you to think through all of the stages of mentoring, whether you are a prospective mentee, mentor or an organiser. Please let us know if you use the book to help set up mentoring schemes or relationships and do tell us of any successes or difficulties that emerge from the process.

Claire Malcolm
Director
New Writing North
claire@newwritingnorth.com

New Writing North is the writing development agency for the north east of England. We aim to create an environment in the North East in which new writing in all forms can flourish and develop. We are a unique organisation within the UK, merging as we do individual development work with writers across all media with educational work and the production of creative projects. We work with writers from different genres and forms to develop career opportunities, new commissions, projects, residencies, publications and live events. For more information about our work, see www.newwritingnorth.com.

Contents

Introduction

What is mentoring?

A good question. Here are some possible answers:

A mentor is 'a person who achieves a one to one developmental relationship with a learner, and one whom the learner identifies as having enabled personal growth'.
Christine Bennett, University of Exeter

[A mentor is] a role model who helps others to achieve their potential.
National Mentoring Network

A one-to-one non-judgmental relationship in which an individual mentor voluntarily gives his/her time to support and encourage another. The relationship is typically developed at a time of transition in the mentee's life, and it lasts for a significant and sustained period.
Home Office, Active Communities Unit

A recognisable process where one person offers help, guidance, advice and support with respect to the learning or development of another person.
Neil Blunt, Arts Training Central

Our own definition, which underpins the work in this book, is:

Mentoring is a process through which someone with expertise and experience in your field of work chooses to support you in a time of transition.

'Mentoring' has become a bit of a buzzword in literature development over the past few years. There are numerous mentoring schemes throughout the UK, set up by various types of organisations, specifically for creative writers. Many of these will be discussed in detail later. Yet there is little agreement about exactly what mentoring *is*; virtually no research on what (if anything) it offers in terms of a writer's professional development; and little coherence about how it might be accessed, managed and delivered. Anecdotally it is clear that writers, both emergent and more experienced, do get a great deal out of mentoring relationships. It may not be necessary at this point to quantify that, and certainly we have no intention of laying down 'rules' about it. None the less, a good deal of money, from public, institutional and private pockets, is being invested in the process and so it is worth exploring what is going on with a view to determining some guidelines for best practice and best value.

The original Mentor was a friend of Odysseus in Homer's *Odyssey*. When Odysseus failed to return from the Trojan War his young adult son, Telemachus, was left in a tricky position: he had neither personal nor professional authority and his household and country needed urgent management – his mother's suitors were creating expensive havoc and Telemachus could not command the support of his own citizens. Mentor became his principal counsellor. More importantly however, Athena, the Goddess of Wisdom, disguised herself as Mentor when she wished to give Telemachus direct advice. She offered her young favourite a number of different things: she provided a human, one-to-one presence (usually advice from the gods was given via dreams, inspiration, omens or prophecy, but this was person-to-person); she boosted his confidence; and she gave him detailed, practical advice, both in general terms about leadership and in immediate and practical terms about what he might *do*.

Some relevant lessons can be derived from this story: a mentor is on your side – it is a non-judgmental relationship and directed towards the less experienced person's own agenda. Mentor had no authority over Telemachus. Telemachus was in a stage of transition. Homer makes clear that their communication was private and confidential. Mentor, after both his real and his 'divine' visit, went away and left Telemachus to get on with the job himself.

Hence the word 'mentor' came to mean, as the *Oxford English Dictionary* puts it, "An experienced and trusted counsellor or advisor." It was used regularly in this context in the nineteenth century – a well-known example is in Louisa May Alcott's *Little Women,* when after a stern but useful reprimand from Amy, Laurie writes to her as "Dear Mentor" and signs himself "Telemachus".

In the 1970s and 80s, mentoring re-emerged as a management training technique. Reg Hamilton in his book *Mentoring – A Manager's Pocket Guide (*The Industrial Society, 1993) suggests that in the USA – where perhaps unsurprisingly mentoring in this form first appeared – this model was given a boost by anti-discrimination legislation. Companies, obliged to promote women and minorities, realised that traditional training strategies did not help those who had less knowledge of management culture or were disadvantaged by low self-esteem or a shortage of role models. A more personal and non-judgmental framework was needed to suit the learning needs of a new group of potential managers. Mentoring developed as a training technique that was one-to-one and individual; was designed to encourage self-confidence and independence (rather than skills teaching); was experiential (responding to actual events on the ground rather than an abstract training scheme); was time limited; and was non-judgmental. (There remains within management training an unresolved tension as to whether or not mentoring should be 'confidential' and whether or not a mentor should have a formal assessment role.)

Within the concept of mentoring in this management context, various approaches and methods have developed. Some of these are worth exploring a little.

Sponsorship systems

Here senior managers make a specific investment in a new recruit; they provide a range of experiences through special projects and assignments; they extend their network to embrace their protégé; they ensure the newcomer is widely recognised within the company by giving him or her exposure and public standing.

Role models

Here the newcomers define their needs and select, or ask senior management to select, mentors for them who are individuals who have already tackled these specific issues successfully. In this approach the managers may well seek mentors outside the organisation itself, and the matching of mentors and mentees has to be done with some precision. There is less emphasis on the 'public face' and more on the mentees gaining insight into themselves and their own development by observing (and critiquing) the mentors' attitudes, values, strategies and general approach. (This model has proved particularly effective for the development of minority groups, who may have had less opportunity to observe a reasonable range of role models in earlier life.)

Management mentoring

Here line managers 'add on' mentoring to their other training strategies. The focus here will be wider than in the other two models – the mentors will have a strategic plan (eg, staff retention; development of minority or other specific groups). They will probably see themselves more as 'coaches' or trainers than as counsellors or advisors.

We have outlined these differences because in our experience when it comes to mentoring for creative writing there is considerable confusion and a tension between various expectations. Many (even most) writers seeking mentoring would favour, consciously or otherwise, a sponsorship approach – they want to get on in this business! Most writers offering mentoring however prefer a role model or personal development focus and project managers have issues of overall strategy and accountability. Thus you can end up with excellent programmes, all calling themselves 'mentoring', with totally different aims and methods. Anne Caldwell ran schemes for the National Association of Writers in Education and the National Association for Literature Development, which were part of a wider professional development programme that also included seminars and other opportunities such as shadowing or placements. In these schemes no writing was addressed at all – it was geared to personal and professional development and to wider career opportunities.

On the other hand, Jill Dawson, who was a mentor in the Writers' Pool scheme which was run by the Royal Literary Fund, is saying exactly the opposite: she comments that mentees can ask for awkward things – such as references, jacket puffs, quotes or introductions to an agent. It is good to write into the contract that such services are excluded. In that way the mentor can refuse them if they are not appropriate without any explanation other than referral back to the contract. It seems to us important that schemes should define, at least to some extent, what it is they believe they are offering.

Meanwhile, within creative writing, mentoring has always existed on an informal level (and frequently on a sponsorship model): Ezra Pound famously took TS Eliot under his wing, both introducing him to many leading writers and publishers and also working with him on his own poetry – his suggestions and comments on the original draft of *The Waste Land* are almost shocking in their level of editorial intervention. Similar mentoring relationships existed between Verlaine and Rimbaud; Graham Greene and Muriel Spark; James Joyce and Samuel Beckett; and Truman Capote and Harper Lee.

In all these cases the relationship was voluntary on both sides, with the mentors offering their services for a range of motives, both artistic and personal. However they are never *professional* relationships in the sense that no one pays anyone, and there are obviously no formal structures or monitoring and evaluation aspects. Of course this particular (and rich) form of friendship continues and will continue, along with co-mentoring (and its modern offshoot – the writers' group), but it is outside the brief of this book. It is probably easier to see and assess the contemporary interest in mentoring for creative writers by looking at how it has grown out of the management techniques discussed above than out of these friendship networks and collegiate generosity.

The rise of mentoring for creative writers has to be seen in the context of a change in the marketplace. Over the last few decades, publishing has become more aggressively commercial – in particular requiring a faster return on capital outlay. Long-term investment in new writers is now harder to justify within mainstream publishing than in the middle of the last century. (*Sara Maitland's first novel in the mid-1970s was commissioned before a single word of it had been written, or even a synopsis created, on the basis of a few published short stories. The support that her publisher provided during the whole process was true 'mentoring'. Unless one is already a public figure this is now more or less unimaginable.*) Far less editing at the creative and draft stages now happens within publishing houses; publishers buy books that are essentially completed and likely to prove profitable *quickly.* At the same time there is an increasing and voracious appetite for new voices. 'New' here means both first-time novelists with highly commercial manuscripts *and* writers from communities not yet heard from in the commercial sector.

It is fairly clear that both these groups are likely to profit from support while they produce these commercially viable manuscripts. This situation has generated a number of supportive 'training' approaches – MAs in creative writing, writers-in-residence, an enhanced role for agents, writing courses, workshops, literary consultancies and so on. Some of these are paid for commercially (or semi-commercially) by individuals, but a good deal of this development work has fallen on the public sector. Arts Council England and its Scottish, Welsh and Northern Irish counterparts for some time have offered bursaries and 'scholarships' or grants in various forms to emerging writers of promise. Welsh literature agency Academi manages a rolling programme of mentoring schemes with open application for writers across Wales twice a year. In Northern Ireland, the Creative Writers Network also manages mentoring schemes. In addition, literature development agencies, along with other publicly subsidised arts organisations, have an increasing remit to work towards a fuller representation of diversity and an anti-discrimination agenda. Not surprisingly then, such organisations (and their funders) look towards models from industry and commerce, which have already begun to tackle exclusion. Some of the earliest mentoring for writers came in those areas where the organisational structures replicated commercial enterprises to a greater or lesser degree. That is to say, there was an 'office' or 'factory', where management and creative roles overlapped and both were 'on-site'– theatres, for example, were among the first organisations to extend mentoring to dramatists.

Shifting mentoring from this original 'management training' model to one designed for the 'off-site' nature of most poets, novelists and short story writers has necessitated radical changes in the forms that mentoring takes, and indeed what it is expected to deliver. These models are still evolving. There has been very little shared practice, no central information exchange and it is extremely hard to discover the full extent of mentoring opportunities or precisely what each organisation can offer. In this book we try to describe and offer examples of different forms of mentoring (and evaluate them) rather than offering a full and comprehensive survey. Here are some prevailing models.

■ **'Private' schemes**. Here there is no manager – would-be mentees select and employ their own mentors. An example of this would be the very successful project between Rosie Lugosi and John Siddique. Lugosi made a bid to Arts Council England to support her writing, with a mentoring element built into the application. When she received a grant, she and Siddique organised and administered the whole package themselves.

■ **Schemes set up by managers to work with a particular (pre-determined) group of potential writers**, eg, women, black and ethnic minority communities, disabled writers, prisoners or writers in a geographical area.

■ **Schemes, like New Writing North's, where the project is managed and funded by a third party** and the mentoring partnerships are set up individually to support particular writers, and the mentors are chosen individually to match those writers. The commercial schemes also tend to work this way, except that the mentees will be paying the mentors themselves (via the management).

■ **Schemes that recruit a group of mentors and select the mentees by a 'competitive' process**. Such schemes will run between pre-arranged dates and tend to have clearer guidelines, assessment criteria and detailed feedback. The Royal Literary Fund scheme, which unfortunately is no longer running, was of this type.

■ **Co-mentoring**. We consider this briefly in the 'Mentees' section and clearly co-mentors can also benefit from the 'Mentors' section of this book. We know of no formalised schemes through which writers can make contact with each other and enter into a formalised co-mentoring agreement, but believe this to be a fruitful area for development.

■ **Others**. There are assorted other schemes – for example, those like the National Association of Writers in Education's project which mentors for professional skills (writers in classrooms, or performance skills for instance) rather than working directly with the writing itself. And there are those schemes that, while based on one of the previous models, deliver in specific ways. Crossing Borders (a joint project of Lancaster University and the British Council) used the competitive recruitment process outlined above, but delivered mentoring to African writers, entirely by email.

In this book, we have divided the material not by type of scheme but by roles within it: mentees, mentors, and managers, because that seems to us more useful and accessible. However, it is important to state that there is still some debate about exactly what mentoring is and the many forms it can take, even within the field of creative writing.

For mentees and emerging writers

"My advice to anyone offered a mentoring opportunity is to go for it, but clear space in your diary so you don't waste it! Mentoring only works if both the mentor and mentee treat it as a serious contract, with a commitment to produce work and feedback, as well as meeting agreed timings.

"There is a real skill in matching people, so an initial meeting is vital before both sides agree to spend so much time working together. Having a mentor gave me a real reason to push away distractions and concentrate on my writing. I wrote and rewrote, I tried so many new things, I read without feeling guilty – it was a very worthwhile experience. I have my mentor's comments and notes in a ring binder and still use them."

Fiona Richie Walker, writer

What is mentoring and is it for you?

What mentoring is

Mentoring is a process through which someone with expertise and experience in your field of work chooses to support you in a time of transition. Mentoring in its modern usage emerged within business management training, but has recently gained popularity in the arts too. Mentoring for writers is usually rather different from the business management model. For example, it does not necessarily include marketing skills or inter-personal management development – it is more likely to be focused on the writing itself. In some ways this makes it closer to the business management concept of 'coaching', but the words 'mentoring' and 'mentor' are now so firmly on the agenda that we are going to use them.

What mentoring isn't

Mentoring isn't editing. It isn't manuscript appraisal. It isn't one writer passing judgment on another. It isn't networking. It isn't a ticket to commercial success. It isn't trying to write like someone else. It isn't befriending. These elements and others may shade the process, but are not the aim of the process. To go back to 'what mentoring is':

Mentoring is a professional relationship with a sympathetic fellow writer, for an agreed period of time, whose focus is your work and how you can raise it to a new level.

The benefits of mentoring

Writing is necessarily an isolated business. The process takes place while sitting at a computer or bending over a sheet of paper, and also when staring through a window.

Mentors help you step beyond that private process. They are professionals in your field, yet they have no need to shape your work according to their own priorities. Most critical readers at this stage – agents, editors or friends – will bring their own agenda to the reading. Mentors are different. They have been through the mill themselves; they have pulled their own writing out of the fire many times.

How does this help you?

Mentors are not likely to attack your writing, or to sit in judgment on it. You may of course get some clear opinion about what doesn't work for the mentor. The mentor's aim, though, is to burrow into your writing process. He or she seeks to understand what it is you are trying to achieve, and then help you to achieve it. The piece of writing you offer your mentor is material for your mentor. Your mentor uses it to find ways to strengthen you as a writer.

You may be lacking in self-confidence. The mentor should leave you feeling better about yourself and also with the evidence to support that.

Why might I want a mentor?

You may want a mentor if you answer yes to at least some of the following questions:

❑ Is my writing at a point of transition?
❑ Have I taken my work as far as I know how, yet know I can move it further somehow?
❑ Am I ready to open up my work to objective scrutiny?
❑ Am I prepared to put my writing through a nine- to twelve-month development process, rather than putting it out into the world now?

You may also answer yes to the following questions:

❑ Are you lonely? Do you find the world of publishing harsh, too commercial, abrasive, unsympathetic? Are you confident of your own genius, and sure that writers in your field will appreciate and promote your work if they give it due consideration?

Your mentor may share the same feelings, but she isn't there to meet those needs in you. These last questions are not ones that should lead to mentoring. Check the questions you are asking and see whether they are the right ones.

When is the right time to seek a mentor?

When you recognise that you are at a point of transition in your work. (Some of the most effective mentoring relationships we have encountered have been between a writer of some experience who wants to shift form – say from poetry to prose fiction – and a mentor experienced in the new form.)

You can afford the time to dedicate to the project. Not just the time for the sessions and dialogue with your mentor, but the writing time you will need to put in between each session.

You have put in a lot of work on your own, and are ready to open your work up to others. You keep making fresh attempts to find your voice, or the voice of a new piece. Are you close, have you been close, or should you make yet another fresh start? A mentor may have the experience and objectivity to guide you.

What happens if you feel you have finished the major draft of a big work, for example a novel? At that point you have stepped beyond a mentor's reach. You can make use of a manuscript appraisal service. However, if what that appraisal gives you is an awareness that the next draft needs something more, something somehow radically different, a mentor might usefully enter the scene. But you may feel you need support and experience at almost any point in the process. For instance (with that novel) you may be struggling with issues of plotting or ending – for those issues too, a mentor may be able to make a useful contribution.

If you've got a great poetry sequence, book, play, film, story or performance piece that you're desperate to bring to the world, this isn't the moment to seek a mentor. The mentoring relationship works best if the mentor is reading new work, and you use the feedback from one session with the mentor to prepare new work for the next one.

At what stage in my writing career should I seek a mentor?

Mentoring has worked very effectively for a great range of people.

However, it is a time-demanding and expensive process, so you do want to be at a point where you will get the most out of it. If you have never written anything before, remember the mentoring process starts with your submitting a piece of your writing. If the material is there for a mentor to engage with, then it can work. You need to get something down on paper to show a potential mentor. Raw enthusiasm is probably not quite enough. Find something to read first, something that speaks to you, and get into the reading habit. You can learn a lot about writing from reading others. Then set yourself a regular slot in which you sit and write something down. Fill some pages. Build up a work habit, a bit of self-discipline. Really give it a go and see if you can come up with something that will attract a mentor or organisation to work with you.

It is usually expected that writers have already reached some level of achievement before mentoring starts, but showing commitment and having something to work with are every bit as important as commercial success.

But mentoring does require both willingness to stretch yourself and some level of basic competence. Punctuation and spelling for example do matter. It is not a mentor's job to provide that sort of *teaching*. If this is a real concern of yours, you might first seek help from a more practical English (or Welsh or Gaelic) language teaching programme or adult literacy course. You probably will need to be able to type – it is hard work trying to decode longhand and few if any mentors will be willing to put in that level of effort.

When more formal educational routes have failed, but you still have a strong urge to write, mentoring may be able to help. You would need your mentor or the sponsoring organisation to be aware of your difficulties and be happy to take them on board. The mentor is not there to edit your work, but might be prepared to note essential details for you to focus on.

Also, you and your mentor might agree that you can break all the rules, that you want your voice to come through unshackled, that you want to write for people who don't care about grammar. If you find a mentor open enough to take on that challenge, one who is excited about what you write, it could work.

Generally though it is best to know the rules, to be able to apply them, before you break them. Punctuation, for example, is partly just the way breath gets marked down on paper. Understand that, work with it, and you may find it helps shape your work so that more people can access it.

Some schemes, such as that run by Academi in Wales, offer opportunities for being mentored in languages other than English. If you want to write in a minority language that does not have the literary models or mentors that you need, it may be possible to work with an English-speaking mentor. You might be mentored in English while also writing your work in another language.

Publishers are looking for voices from communities that are new to them. Mentoring might help you fit your material into the sort of structure they are used to and are looking for. Try to find a mentor who is open to any new way you might want to use the language. So long as you are consistent in the choices you make, you can work on bringing new dialect into English.

Another effective type of mentoring is for writers who want to shift from one form to another. For example, novelists who would like to write plays or poets who wish to develop their prose fiction. The usual thing here is to work with a writer who is more at home with both the new form and its professional requirements. These are often very positive and happy relationships on both sides, perhaps because both parties feel a natural 'equality' and respect.

"Having a mentor has been invaluable to me as a poet starting out on the long journey of writing a novel. I have been mentored before, as a poet, and found that experience very useful. This time round the major difference is my mentor has been supporting me while I confront the issues inherent in such a major switch of genres. At times my novel simply felt so long that I could not continue. My mentor helped me to contextualise what I'm trying to do and give me some perspective on a creative process that is very new to me. We have looked at technical aspects of craft, plot and story and I now feel better equipped to move forward.

"When I started this novel, I did not even know if I could finish it. One of the most valuable things I have learned during my mentorship is that I do want to continue, and that I might just be able to do it. For a poet, that's a big leap into a lot of words."
Lisa Matthews, writer

What is the role of the mentor?

The mentor engages with your writing.

Mentors blend criticism and encouragement. Essentially they help you to write to your strengths, perhaps by bringing them to your notice for the first time. Once you know your strengths, they can help you correct structural elements that might be weaknesses. For example, ruminant digressions may work well if your skill rests in evoking the natural world, and less so if your strength is narrative drive.

Mentors should keep you on track. Their comments may be challenging. The relationship only works if you accept those challenges, but challenges can be hard to accept. The mentor is stubborn and supportive in keeping you to the task – and encourages every sign of success.

Mentors listen – and prompt you with questions about your own writing process so that they have something worthwhile to listen to.

Mentors help place you in the context of a larger writing community. In the first place, they do this by giving you their own regard. Subsequently they can direct your reading, and relate your writing to the writing of others.

Mentors maintain the flow of communication between you, keep you informed of any changes in the programme or timing, and prompt you if necessary.

Mentoring is an interactive process, but the mentors are responsible for bringing the programme to a successful completion where possible.

Occasionally mentors might offer you a rewrite of a certain passage. Seeing a model of a different way can often be helpful in breaking new ground.

Mentors might listen to your personal history, and refer you elsewhere if necessary, but their main task will be to help you work out any problems you might have with your writing by focusing on your writing. They are not therapists.

Mentors are there to listen, to suggest, to point you to boundaries that you might choose to break through, to strengthen your craft, to increase your range of skills, to broaden your horizons and sharpen your ambitions.

Will mentoring change my life?

It is a serious commitment over a lengthy and sustained period of time. It may mean giving up your weekends. It may mean someone else agreeing to take over a portion of the domestic load, such as washing up or looking after the children. You are committing yourself to a sustained creative process, which is likely to bring an element of turmoil to your life. Is your life balanced enough to sustain those added emotional shifts? Are the important people in your life able to understand and support you? Can you create a quiet, safe space and regular timeslots in which to sit and work?

Writing at this level is likely to touch something elemental in your life. Your relationship with your mentor may take on meaning way beyond the reality: 'At last someone understands me!' This can be both exciting and risky.

In deciding to go into a mentoring process, it might be a good idea to abandon all other decisions for the period. Don't sell the house or buy another. Don't get divorced or break up with friends. Don't give up your job. Give yourself to the writing process and leave the rest of life on track as much as possible. Wait at least three months after the end of the mentoring period before doing anything crazy. Writing is crazy enough.

On the other hand, mentoring can offer some mutual flexibility in a way that most learning opportunities cannot. If you are ill, for instance, it is usually possible to reschedule meetings or deadlines by mutual agreement.

I have mobility problems (or live in the middle of nowhere) so I cannot meet with a mentor. Is there anything I can do?

Mentoring can be done, and has been done, online. The only difference is that the 'meetings' become email exchanges. Some people believe that mentoring works *better* online than face-to-face. There are three reasons why this might be the case:

■ You get better 'value for money' as nothing (including time) has to be spent on travel and meeting arrangements.

■ So many (irrelevant) personal issues can be discounted. It won't matter if your mentor's smoking habits would make you feel sick, or your dress sense grates on her nerves. It is easier to absorb criticism and respond when you are ready – rather than flaring up before you have had time to think. Two people do not have to match their diaries precisely.

■ Using writing to explore writing – to express sensitive feelings, for example, without the back-up of tone, gesture and body language – allows you an extra opportunity to develop nuance, subtlety and sophistication. This obviously can strengthen your 'real' writing.

Of course there are arguments on the other side too, but particularly for those writers who could not easily find a 'local' mentor it is a choice well worth considering.

I'm a rule breaker. It sounds like mentoring comes with rules attached. Should I steer clear of it?

Writers tend to be rule breakers. One advantage of mentoring is that it is separate from formal educational systems. If you're considering taking up a mentoring scheme, you're already thinking about shaping your work to meet an audience (even if it is only an audience of one – the mentor), so already you are showing some willingness to compromise.

The basic rules are about effort, timekeeping and communication. So long as you can hold to those, you needn't worry. Mentoring is about helping you towards breakthroughs, not about making you comply.

Can mentoring work for shy people?

Writing is a solitary pursuit. The results of putting writing into the world can be bruising, so it is tempting to keep it to oneself. However, the focus of mentoring is on the writing, not on the writer. If the sample you submit attracts a mentor to work on it, then mentoring is for you. Welcome out of your shell. Know the mentor is there to care for you as you develop, and enjoy the process of opening out a little.

Maybe mentoring – but what are the other options?

What are the alternatives to finding myself a mentor?

■ Join a writers' group.

■ Join an online writing community.

■ Work with a creative writing book, such as Sara Maitland's *The Writer's Way* or the 'Teach Yourself' series.

■ Take a preliminary writing course. Check what is on offer from your local further education college or university or public library. An adult education option is available for most people.

■ There are online creative writing courses, such as those offered by Trace (at Nottingham Trent University) and Cardiff University. And there are more traditional 'correspondence courses' like those of the Open College of the Arts or The Writers' Bureau. (If you are interested in this approach do be sure to check very carefully that the course you are signing up for, and paying for, is really going to offer what you want.)

■ Take a residential course, like those run by the Arvon Foundation.

■ Share your work with a fellow writer and take it in turns to comment on and shape each other's work.

■ Send your manuscript to a manuscript appraisal service. This may well be your best bet if you have finished your work and are looking for professional feedback. Mentoring works best when a project is fresh and ongoing.

■ Find/create opportunities to read your work in public.

■ Write for a local market that you can reach (through self-publication of local interest material or articles in the local press) and gain confidence and feedback from readers. Walking guides, cycling guides, pub guides, local history, local family trees – all give real experience of writing yet don't require the same burning creative process.

■ Take an MA in creative writing. These can be done full- or part-time, and some of them have a distance learning option (eg, Lancaster University, Manchester Metropolitan University, De Montfort University, Newcastle University and The Open University).

How does an MA in creative writing compare with mentoring?

One obvious difference is the academic requirements of entry. MA courses are flexible, and some students are accepted without an initial degree, but these are rare instances. The courses themselves need to fit within the university's parameters of what a course should look like, with the appropriate modules. Given that, Harriett Gilbert says of the MA in novel writing she runs at City University, London:

"So far as is compatible with a degree course, literary theory is kept to the sidelines. Students read widely and discuss novels, but look at the works as though they were by fellow novelists. Written work is journalistic, in essay form aimed at the broadsheet newspapers, so made to be readable and without footnotes. The pragmatism of the journalism department feeds into the programme. Students are required to finish a novel as part of the course. The thinking behind that is that you must know how you can finish a novel. Another aim is to work out how to build a career of which novel writing is one strand, accepting that students are unlikely to live off writing. Candidates' thoughts on this are checked at interview, and they are disabused of the notion that novel writing is a way to earn a lot of money. The course is run part-time, in the evenings and at occasional weekends, for students who have to work in order to support the course. They fit the course in around their working lives, and most students will in fact finish a decent novel.

"Students gain considerably from workshop sessions. From term three of the course, workshops are voluntary, but the majority of students get together once every two weeks. They email chapters and points around to each other, or just meet, but they maintain email contact constantly.

"Most come to the course *for* the group feedback. In interview, most candidates have been on Arvon or adult education courses, and positively enjoyed the workshop experience. Students workshop exercises set by the tutor, on such things as character development. For example, they might be given a photograph and be asked to develop a character from it and write a scene. For dialogue, they might be asked to listen and transcribe what people actually say, then see how the verbatim words become stylised and transformed in text. They might look at what is meant by resolving plot, and what contract writers make with the reader. That can also be saved for the private sessions with the tutor. Characters developed in exercises often find their way into a novel.

"Students start off needing deadlines, whipping, comfort and reassurance, but after nine months they know where they are going with the novel. They are writing faster, and some students ask to be given deadlines. Work is submitted in 10,000 word tranches. The tutor gives the copy back with notes written upon it. In tutorials, the student talks first and the tutor holds back for as long as possible. Students write within their own easy parameters. They need pushing into something different, to do things they don't naturally do. After the final module, students take part in a showcase, giving readings to an invited audience."

An alternative take on the differences between mentoring schemes and MA courses comes from Jill Dawson, who managed The Writers' Pool mentoring scheme for the Royal Literary Fund. After extensive work both as a mentor and as a tutor on MA courses, she found that mentoring was preferable:

"MA students can be unrealistic about those who teach them. If they sign up to a course in order to be with a 'named' author, the reality is that they will only have four half-hour sessions with that author during the course. They tend not to appreciate the extent to which the other students on their course offer a valuable resource. It was a similar situation on the Arvon courses, when students thought they would have more individual input. In fact they would only be seen once, or maybe twice, by the writer whose name attracted them.

"I often have to read a piece of work many, many times, particularly if it is a very good piece of work which I don't immediately have anything to say about. With 12 students, rather than the select few of mentoring, it's possible to get sloppy and slapdash. It's only human nature not to do it so thoroughly. With a novel there *is* a period of natural ebb and flow, and anxiety when nothing happens. A mentee might go away from a session inspired, filled with ideas, yet run into a block about how to actually impart those ideas into the writing. Weeks might pass with nothing happening, then one night there is a flash of inspiration and the novel pours through again. Working with that process is very interesting. However on a course where students are required to produce work, that ebb and flow isn't catered for. If they don't meet deadlines, they fail. New writers often have fantasies about writing 1,000 words a day. One of the mentor's jobs is to correct that fantasy.

"When students are working in a group of 12, even when the course has been set up so that feedback is constructive, there is a difference between the diffident students and the confident ones. When students are delivering their opinions on a piece of work, the diffident ones tend to absorb it rather than challenge it. In a one-to-one situation it is possible to say, 'this is just my opinion' – and it is good when mentees subsequently don't do what you suggest. It is important that they feel ownership of their own writing. Writing is not a group or consensual activity. Students must be tough and hold out for what they think is good about their own work."

The manuscript appraisal alternative

When Becky Swift set up leading UK manuscript appraisal service The Literary Consultancy in 1996, little support was available to writers. There were a few editors you could pay to consider your manuscript, but such work was stigmatised and not thought to be honourable.

When she worked at Virago, Swift was hurt to see the size of the slush pile. She was also struck by the ignorance of people submitting work, yet upset and anxious about their not receiving thoughtful responses. When an editor did dare respond, the writers would never let them go. When editors do decide against a book it's not their job to spike the writer's fantasies. Her concept for The Literary Consultancy, which she still runs, is that it offers a short, sharp shock. It dares to give an opinion. Letting go of a manuscript is important, and her work can be about helping people to let go.

The Literary Consultancy develops, creates and maintains links with literary agents, so that it is poised to give advice when something is good. If there is anything hopeful in a work, then they are in a good position to identify it. If not, then it is good for writers to learn to deal with a tough response, and to understand the thought process behind it. It is better to hear an unpleasant truth than to go round in a fog of being encouraged. A real writer will find some way of using any response.

Mentoring puts a thoughtful person in touch with a good writer. To choose a mentoring path means a writer has taken a decision that they want to commit. Being a writer is a vocational calling. However, The Literary Consultancy caters for a massive range of absolute beginners who don't want mentoring. They want a one-off reflection on what they've done.

OK, let's go for it. How do I get started?

How do I find a mentor?

Once you are certain that you do want and could use a mentor there are various ways of proceeding:
- You can apply to take part in a mentoring scheme, an organised mentoring process set up by a literature or arts organisation.
- You can approach one of the commercial mentoring services.
- You can set up your own private and individual mentoring relationship.
- You can think about the possibilities of co-mentoring.

Probably the very first thing to do is to go and talk through your project with a local literature development officer. Literature development is handled in different ways in different regions of the country – but a literature or theatre officer at the regional office of Arts Council England, Academi in Wales, The Arts Council of Northern Ireland or The Scottish Arts Council would be a good starting point.

Many local councils also have a literature development officer, who will be able to tell you about any mentoring schemes in your area and, if appropriate, discuss with you the possibility of making a funding application. They should also be able to point you towards organisations that offer mentoring to specific groups. There are particular funding streams to open up arts participation to sections of the community who have not been fully represented. Playwrights are particularly well served in this respect. On the whole, however, these schemes are run occasionally as one-off projects and you need to be in the right place at the right time – if this is appropriate to you, make sure you establish good contact with your development officer, and get yourself on the mailing list of appropriate organisations so they can let you know when these opportunities are coming up. Literature development officers may also be able to recommend writers who are experienced mentors or who are interested in working in this way.

Mentoring schemes
These schemes are funded; the individual writer will not have to pay for the mentoring. They are also competitive; the organisers choose mentees from among the applicants. It is worth finding out what the particular criteria for selection are before you apply. For example, the

scheme might be designed, as suggested above, for a specific group – there have been schemes targeted at the ethnic minority community, women, deaf writers, prisoners, teenagers and so on. Alternatively, a scheme might be specifically directed at particular forms (novels, poetry, dramatists etc) or be designed to support writers at a particular point in their career: for example, to invest in those considered nearly ready to publish; or in experienced writers wanting to move form or shift their career in a particular direction; or the organisers might be keen to select writers who have not had the opportunity to get so far. Some schemes are planned to enhance professional opportunities for writers and some are entirely focused on text. Obviously it is sensible to look at these factors before applying – and to clarify for yourself what your goals are, and where you stand in career terms.

In these schemes the managing agency will take responsibility not just for choosing the mentees, but also for selecting the mentors and matching them to mentees, monitoring the process and mediating if things go wrong. They will support both you and the mentor and may provide firm guidelines about the timing and the frequency of meetings, the amount of writing you should be submitting and the sort of feedback you will be offered. Many of these schemes will require you to enter into some form of formal contract. They may also arrange induction days and facilitate exchange between members of the scheme.

It is very affirming to be selected for any such scheme, but it is still crucial that you check the proposed details, see if they match your own needs and that you understand and can accept the 'rules'. At the end of this book, there is a list of organisations that deliver mentoring.

Commercial mentoring

Recently we have seen the emergence of commercial mentoring services – these will set up partnerships with appropriate mentors and monitor the process for you, for a fee. Since such organisations work nationally they are likely (though not exclusively) to do so on a distance-learning model.

These services are relatively new in the UK and none yet has a strong track record: we have not been able to talk to anyone who has used one of them to access mentoring. However, they are well established in the USA, where they have real fans. If you are thinking about using this sort of provision, try starting with a web search so you can make some informed comparisons.

At this stage we would caution against paying up front for a whole mentoring process. We feel that payment should be phased over the duration of the mentoring.

The organisation should also offer you a contract that makes clear what is expected from you in terms of material delivered and dates; what the mentor will deliver and in what form; and what happens in the event of a breakdown in the mentoring relationship – do they offer a mediation process, and what are you liable for if such mediation is not effective?

Some individual writers set up mentoring services, which are essentially a commercial framework for themselves as sole traders. These have lower infrastructure costs than the larger organisations, and so might be cheaper. On the other hand, they offer no third party to help keep things running smoothly, and do not have the wider pool of writers available from which to draw the most suitable match for you.

These commercial organisations are generally very approachable by phone and willing to talk about how they might meet your needs. There is no reason why you cannot use this guide to help you work out your own ideal model of mentoring and how much you are prepared to pay for it, and then see if they are able to provide such a service. Mentoring is interactive; as a mentee you are being accompanied, not instructed. Feel free to try and negotiate a service that meets your needs.

Private mentoring

There is nothing to stop you contacting any writer you think you might like to work with and asking them to be your mentor. You should send a *short* sample of your writing with your letter – probably not more than 5,000 words of prose or half a dozen poems – and you should briefly outline your goals. If you take this bold approach it is probably sensible to assure them early in the letter that you are willing to pay for this service; it is probably polite to approach them initially through their agent or publisher. It is certainly sensible to be prepared for rejection.

Perhaps a safer approach would be to approach a writer you have met – perhaps the facilitator of a workshop you have attended or the tutor on a course you have taken. You could also ask the literature development officers we mentioned above if they could recommend particular writers who are experienced mentors or who are interested in working in this way. Remember there are no formal qualifications for mentoring in the UK – and there is very little training at present, although some writers may have undergone some induction, or have previous experience.

When you approach a potential mentor in this direct way you will be proposing to employ someone directly – you will be both manager and client. At least initially you will have to take the lead in the negotiations.

Many writers who are willing to act as mentors prefer to do it through a 'third party' as this feels more professional and less intrusive. It is up to you to reassure them that you are professional and mature enough not to be an excessive drain on their time and attention, and that you have thought through the implications.

Naturally, anyone you approach as a potential mentor will expect to see something of your work before they agree. Mentoring can only work well if the mentors find something in your writing that chimes with their own work and interests. But they will also be encouraged if you can express your aims and needs and suggest a reason why you have selected them.

It is probably worthwhile drafting an outline contract to offer them – subject obviously to negotiations *(see the sample Mentoring Agreement at the end of this book).* This should outline your proposed timescale, the number of meetings and the amount of writing you propose to submit before each meeting.

You should also have thought through the question of payment. You are asking to buy not just time but a range of skills and experience. If only to honour your own writing future, you must be able and willing to pay for this properly. One successful fee structure we have seen was based on one full day's recommended writer's pay for every meeting – at present this is £200-£250 – even though the meeting did not last all day. Both parties felt that this was a fair way of paying for preparation and thinking time as well as the meeting itself. You will also need to clarify how you will pay – the mentor is entitled to check that you can afford the service, and the two of you will need to negotiate how the money is to be divided and what happens if, for example, either of you fails to attend an agreed meeting, or if the relationship breaks down.

A normal mentoring cycle will cost at least £1,000 and very likely more. Recently, Arts Council England has given grants to newer writers to employ mentors (usually in conjunction with a bursary to buy the writer some time to work). Look on their website under Grants for the Arts. In all the successful applications we have looked at, the applicant went to the Arts Council with the mentor already on board. You could seek the help of a literature/theatre officer to find such a mentor before making a formal application.

Rosie Lugosi, a poet who wanted to develop her prose fiction, set up a private mentoring contract, and here describes the whole process:

"I met my mentor, John Siddique, via Commonword – a community writing/publishing organisation based in Manchester. As part of a residency, John mentored an 'advanced poets' group. I was one of them, and John and I hit it off immediately. I relished his style, and realised I was getting stacks of positive benefit from our meetings. This was because I very much wanted mentoring input. (I had already applied to the Royal Literary Fund's Writers' Pool, but wasn't successful.) It came at the right time for me in my writing career, and it came in the shape of the right person.

As the residency neared its close I discussed the idea of continuing the mentoring relationship after the three-month period. John was just as eager as me, praise the Lord.

"Which leads us to the plan. Right from the start, it was understood by both of us that John would be paid, and be paid at the going rate (I checked with the Society of Authors, and used that as a baseline). This mutual respect was crucial to the mentoring relationship. This was a cornerstone of our good practice.

"So I put together a funding application to Arts Council England, North West: 'Time to Write with Mentoring Support'. This was for £7,000: £5,000 for me, and £2,000 for John. John and I worked together on the application; indeed, he mentored me to write it well! Naturally, John was going to benefit from a successful grant application (which concentrates the mind wonderfully), but the way he supported me to believe I was worthy of the grant was truly esteem-boosting.

In the application we set out a 10-month plan of what we hoped to achieve, including the number of meetings, and a structure of phone and email back-up meetings.

John insisted that he was paid the full day-rate per mentoring meeting, however long the meeting lasted (and they varied from under three hours to five). At first I worried that I wasn't getting enough meetings for my money (I had thought that a short meeting might count as a half-day). However, I never felt short-changed, due to the energy, preparation and care John put into the meetings. I paid John in two instalments: one at the beginning of the period, one half-way through. The money was paid by the Arts Council into my business account, so there was no confusion as to where the money was.

"We stuck pretty much to the original plan. It gave us a sense of structure. The only real change was that we stretched things out. The flexibility we allowed ourselves felt and feels wise. It helped me to feel less pressured. Both of us had personal issues crop up and we allowed ourselves to go easy – but we liked meeting up so much we instituted occasional lunches and coffee!

"I am sure that I would *not* have had the same quality of concentration if this had been a straight bursary. I know myself well enough to say that! I'd have drifted off track, found things other than writing my novel to fill up the extra days, and quite probably lost my initial confidence and direction. This has worked for me. I need something to keep me on track... I have found that the one-to-one energy of a mentoring relationship fuels me very well indeed.

"It suits my work ethic to have deadlines ('Oh God, I must have that chapter ready for John by Thursday!'). I respond well to being a 'good girl' and getting my 'homework' in on time. I don't indulge in self-sabotage, I don't play headgames with my mentor, pushing them into getting angry with me (yawn), I don't act out my childhood trauma by being a rebellious teenager (double yawn). Hell, I've paid for this; I'll get out precisely what I put in.

"If any writers out there know themselves well enough to realise they tend to 'act out', then it's possible a mentoring relationship won't work for them."

Positive/important qualities of my mentor, in no particular order:
- The respect I have for his work.
- The respect I have for his way of working.
- The difference between our artforms: prose and poetry.
- A good personality 'fit'.
- The belief he has in me.
- The belief he has in my work.
- His ability to kick me/entice me out of ruts.
- He challenges me to work differently to my regular 'style'.
- He encourages me to work hard, but also knows when to stop pushing.
- His energy and hard work invested in me. He is not lazy.
- His reliability.
- He is not afraid to criticise constructively. I'm not afraid to listen.
- He is not afraid to praise when it's due. I'm learning to hear it!

"I have kept a separate notebook of our meetings – this includes the writing exercises he set, suggestions he made, feedback and comments he made on chapters of the novel I sent him, plus returned chapters with his scribbles and comments.

"John is generous enough to admit that he has gained creatively from our mentoring relationship. We have already agreed to continue as a co-mentoring relationship when the Arts Council funding comes to an end. I am very much looking forward to this. It feels a marvellous creative opportunity."
Rosie Lugosi

Co-mentoring
You can learn a lot about your own writing by taking on the role of mentor to someone else. Co-mentoring is when you agree to mentor someone else, in exchange for their mentoring you.

Since you are both probably eager to develop your work, you might mentor each other simultaneously. Follow the rules here about timetabling, setting yourself goals, taking notes etc.

If you are co-mentoring, make sure you do not confuse your roles. Make sure to complete one session as either mentor or mentee before switching roles. If you're meeting face-to-face, switching seats at this point can help, so the mentor always sits in the 'mentor's seat'.

Co-mentoring can work especially well if you are trying to switch forms – so poets and novelists, for example, might mentor each other.

When you seek to apply constructive criticism to someone else's work, you are doing so from a perspective outside the creative process. The skills you gain are likely to transfer themselves to your own work, so that you can position yourself at a more critical and less emotional distance when you set about your redrafting process.

When emerging writers give feedback from creative writing courses they often say the part they enjoyed most was the workshops. By workshops, they mean those sessions in which writers took turns engaging with each other's work. Co-mentoring is essentially a mini-workshop run on a sustained basis, following mentoring guidelines, between just two people. They can work well in distance-learning mode – you might seek out a co-mentoring partner by placing an advert in a writing magazine or placing a request in an online forum. If you choose someone who is also a friend, it is a good idea to follow the guideline of not meeting in each other's homes but in some neutral venue, such as a café. This separates the mentoring relationship from the friendship one.

Who makes a good mentor?

Someone who engages with your writing. Someone who has solid experience of the writing process and has thought about this self-consciously and is articulate about it. Someone you like enough but not too much. Someone widely read in your chosen genre or form. Someone whose own writing you admire, but do not wish to copy. Someone who enjoys the process. To be able to be all those things, a good mentor will nearly always be someone who has been published themselves, and is likely to be someone with some experience of teaching creative writing – whether within an educational institution or through delivering workshops.

'Nearly always' obviously raises some questions. There are special cases and they are worth thinking about. Experience has taught that mentoring for playwrights is most useful when it incorporates some opportunity for performance, or for working on the performance elements of a play or script: here a director or dramaturg might make an excellent mentor. Another example would be someone who wanted to create storybooks for younger children, where the elements of illustration and design run parallel to the text. Here perhaps a designer, or indeed someone who works with children in some capacity, might have a great deal to offer as a mentor. For songwriters, a musician might be the best mentor.

Do I need a mentor who is like me?

Many studies say that you don't. There's no need to match for gender, race, faith, sexuality, age or whatever – the results can be the same whatever the mix.

So long as your mentor is open, and you are open, it should work. Women can work with men, lesbians can mentor straight men, your mentor can be younger than you, Asians can work with Caucasians. Mentors are likely to be more alert to writing from experience that is different from their own.

None the less, when problems do come up it is useful to look at whether these are structural – some studies from business management suggest, for example, that women do better with women mentors, although this may not apply within the writing community.

There are real cultural differences about what constitutes 'good writing' and its social uses between various communities. This means that there can be tensions around race between mentors and mentees. Clearly, mentors and mentees may individually be racist or sexist and this could be a barrier to useful mentoring, but very often what is needed is a 'cultural exchange' of information.

If you sense some clash between your mentor and your personal standpoint, go back to the primary rule of mentoring: communicate. Sometimes a little instruction from you can do the trick. Mentors are professionals but we're all learning about life. When the authors of this book were working on Crossing Borders, the mentors worked with about 300 emergent writers over three years. There was only one serious breakdown of communication that seemed to be based on 'differences' between the mentor and the mentee, both of whom felt that the other did not fully respect their standpoint. This situation was resolved by improving communication and by getting both parties to be more direct about their problems.

Should I spend time getting to know the mentor's work?

There's no 'should' involved, but it's a decent thing to do. Also you will find it much easier to get through those times when you feel protective about your own writing, when you are resistant to your mentor's suggestions, if you respect the mentor's work. The mentor will have taken you on because she found something that 'clicked' when she read your work, something that she responded to. It makes sense that this level of respect is mutual.

Mentors are not trying to turn you into duplicates of themselves. Their aim is to help you realise your own unique potential. So when you read the mentor's work, don't view it as a model for your own. It's enough to know that the reader in yourself is fully engaged.

Part of the skill of improving your writing, however, is learning how to read as a writer. Note what your responses are to a piece of writing, then pause and reflect on how those responses were achieved. How did the writer earn that response? Your mentoring process is a unique time in which you could work with a writer to tease out such 'tricks of the trade' and maybe apply them to your own work in some way.

Mentoring is interactive. No writer minds having her work appreciated in professional detail. Flattery, when artfully applied, can boost many relationships, so why not give it a go?

Is the mentor always paid?

Mentoring is a personal dialogue with an expert in your field about your writing and your aspirations for it. Of course this is not a brand new relationship – as we suggested in the introduction, supportive friendships between new and more experienced writers have always existed. But in the present we are talking about a structured approach to providing access to those contacts and opening the process up more widely. Mentoring should be a professional relationship, and mentors will be paid for their services – normally money, unless you have some services you are able to swap.

Can I do a 'swap' instead of paying?

Conceivably, you might have skills you can trade, and you could approach a mentor with, say, £1,000-worth of these. What skills might a writer need? Website design, marketing, reflexology, foreign language tuition, book-keeping. Whatever your own areas of professional expertise, there could be a writer who would benefit from them. Gardening, house-repair, childminding – these might also be barter, but it is worth bearing in mind that many writers are extremely sensitive about their privacy and time and may not want to mix the domestic with the professional in this way.

Getting engaged

What's the next stage after finding my mentor?

Once you have found a mentor and agreed the outlines of your work together, you will need to finalise the contract. This should lay out the expectations on both sides – how long the mentoring will last for, how many meetings are expected, how much contact (by phone or email) is acceptable outside the meetings, how the work you do together will be evaluated and how it will be paid for. There is a sample Mentoring Agreement at the end of this book. If you are entering into a private mentoring relationship take special care to look through the Agreement, seeing if it meets your requirements and discussing it with your prospective mentor. Obviously, each mentoring partnership will have slightly different needs, but the Agreement indicates the things you ought to think about.

Now you are ready to begin. Get out your diaries to find mutually acceptable times and places for the meetings (or deadlines for sending in your writing if you are working online). A good option is to choose meetings that are six weeks apart. That gives you time to incorporate input from one session into your new writing, and submit the new piece in plenty of time for your mentor to consider it. It's usually best to meet in a place such as a café rather than in one of your homes.

How do I set my goals?

At the first meeting, if you have not already done so, you should set out your goals. These may shift during the course of the mentoring period, but they will be goals you accept and probably devise for yourself in discussion with your mentor. (A fine goal is simply to become more conscious and articulate about your own writing process. A mentor's reflections on your work should help you gain a fresh perspective of your own.)

You may be clear about your writing needs and bring specific questions to your mentor. You may simply be stuck and not know how to move forward, in which case the mentor may be the one posing questions. Your writing may be flowing but you wonder if it is on target, if anyone will ever 'get it'.

How do I get the most out of the mentoring process?

Make sure you are both clear about what you expect of each other before you start working together. Be realistic about this.

Be an active partner in the process. Make sure you create the time in between sessions, so that your writing keeps getting better.

If you have issues to raise at a meeting, it is a good idea to write them down beforehand. In the intimacy of meeting, it can sometimes be a help to have a piece of paper to focus on instead of the other person's eyes. Also you can take time out from the flow of your dialogue to check that the questions you brought with you have all been dealt with.

Make notes about your writing process. For example, what are you trying to do that's new for you? How well do you think you achieved it? What is proving particularly difficult? The more self-awareness you can bring to the writing process, the more constructive this mentoring time will be. Don't just leave your mentor to guess at what you are trying to do. Tell her.

It is good to take notes from your meetings. Your mentor might supplement these with handwritten notes made on your draft.

At the end of a meeting, take ten minutes to summarise it together. Make notes of the main points that have been raised, and what actions you might take before the next meeting.

You might gather notes at the end of each writing session in between your submissions of work and your meetings. What was hard? What particular challenges did you set yourself? What pleased you especially? These will be of help to the mentor when they are submitted alongside your work.

Meet the deadlines. And if you can't for any reason, get in touch with your mentor in good time and explain what's happening. Some flexibility should be built into the programme, but it only works so long as both sides keep talking to each other to sort things out.

If you don't understand something, ask questions. If you disagree with something, say so and explain why.

If you feel offended or upset by the mentor's comments, take a deep breath. Give it time. Comments are generally directed at the writing, not at you. Detach yourself. Try to see your writing from your mentor's perspective.

If the mentor suggests new techniques that you are unsure of, try them out. We all put up barriers that are hard to break. Break them. You can always go back to how you were before if you don't like the way things turn out.

Remember that your mentor leads a busy life outside the relationship with you. Try not to impose on her outside your schedule.

What is a good timeframe for mentoring?

Mentoring usually has a set timeframe, probably between nine months and a year. During that period, you and your mentor will meet to discuss your writing. You will agree the timetable between yourselves, but experience suggests that every four to eight weeks usually works well. The meetings may be anywhere, or even 'virtual', using the Internet.

A good basic model to work from is a sequence of six meetings over nine months, spaced six weeks apart. This allows you a month or so to absorb and implement your mentor's responses, before submitting the new writing sample in time for it to be considered.

How many words or poems should I submit before each session?

This depends on your chosen form and needs to be discussed and agreed individually between you and your mentor.

Some mentors like to read a whole work, quite often later on in the mentoring period. Obviously this will not lead to detailed editorial comments, but a more sweeping overview. If the work is substantial, many partnerships agree to treat this as two sessions rather than one.

However, most schemes set boundaries and what follows are averages of those, to give you a general overview:

■ If you're writing in prose, unless you are choosing a highly condensed form akin to poetry, look for a minimum of 1,500 words and a maximum of 3,500. That might be a complete short story, an essay, an episode of a memoir, or a section of a novel or non-fiction work.
■ Poets might offer six poems, or one long poem or poem sequence.
■ Dramatists might offer ten to twenty pages.
■ Performance writers might offer a piece of 10-20 minutes. (As a rough guide, 2,500 words will take 15 minutes to read aloud.)

Occasionally, you and your mentor might decide it would be more useful to present an outline, a proposal or a wider discussion of the work in hand rather than an actual piece of writing. Or a mentor might suggest trying something less obviously connected to the specific work you are dealing with. ("Try writing this idea as a poem"; "What about working on dialogue by experimenting with a radio play?")

The writing should not normally be a first draft, and should have taken a good portion of the writing period between meetings.

Don't enter the process believing you will get most value from the *quantity* of material you submit. Often the meeting can work better if it is tightly focused on a short section of work.

Agreeing boundaries

Certain details, such as frequency of meetings and the length of your submissions before each meeting may be best settled in a contract between the two parties.

Mentoring is a professional association. Writers are vulnerable creatures. Do your best to keep the dialogue to the subject of writing. This isn't the place to bring in personal and social issues. You may well need to explain how these are intruding into your writing time and content, but always seek to bring the focus back to the professional standpoint.

Be on time with your submissions and your meetings. If you cannot be on time, communicate this in advance.

Remember that you are one element in the mentor's working life. Try not to bother the mentor outside your timetabled schedule. Ultimately you are building up your strengths so that the mentoring relationship is no longer needed. Accept the time between submissions as private time in which you are developing your craft.

One particularly delicate issue worth bringing into the open as soon as possible is whether your mentor agrees to promote you 'professionally' – for example, introducing you to agents or editors, inviting you to participate in their readings, arranging meetings with producers, soliciting theatre commissions on your behalf or providing references for you. Overall, we feel that it is unreasonable to expect this in advance – your work may develop in unexpected ways, but, perhaps more importantly, even apparently very successful writers will be nourishing their professional relationships very tenderly for themselves and may be, sensibly, nervous about putting any pressure on their own contacts. Other sorts of support – suggesting competitions you might enter, places you might submit, helping you prepare synopses, proposals or applications, explaining the various 'business' roles – such as, what does an agent *do*? – may be more appropriate. The Royal Literary Fund mentoring contract explicitly excluded professional advice. You may of course raise this with a potential mentor, but do not take it personally if they decline to commit themselves to this. It is much more agreeable and affirming to receive offers of help (if they are forthcoming) at the end of the process. They will be sincere, and you will be grateful!

A publisher's view of mentoring

What might a publisher say about this view that mentoring is there to help you discover your own unique voice, rather than to unpick the secrets of getting published? Ben Ball gave this interview while a senior editor at Simon & Schuster UK. He has since been appointed publisher of Penguin Australia.

Mentoring for creative writers is new on the scene. What are the changes in publishing that might have created this niche?

Publishers are trying to get more out of fewer resources. Editors don't have as long to spend on books as in some recent golden age. More and more people want to write books. We should be publishing fewer books. The funnel gets narrower and everybody's time is tenser. With literary fiction, you do have to hit the ground running.

In contemporary publishing, people have to make it big with their first book or not at all. This isn't so much publishers' doing as people's. People are interested in new things, young things, rather than a body of work. Now publishers have access to sophisticated tracking systems that give them accurate sales figures for all titles, it's much more difficult to overcome a poor track record than no track record. It's better to write a bad book and not publish it than publish it.

How can mentoring help writers be published?

Education is so hit and miss nowadays. Writers need time to work out their minds more. They need another forum in which they can do that. Mentoring is one such forum.

What should mentoring focus on?

Mentoring is not about developing a writer's presentational skills. It's about stripping away the stuff that gets in the way of what you've really got to say. For literary works, mentors should train writers to find their own voice. What's interesting about your book is that it is different to others.

Mentors can be pro-active and find the people that don't know they're writers yet. They can reach the communities that don't have people to express their voices. If voices came out of communities that hadn't formally expressed themselves and they were coherent, publishers would be over the moon. That's exactly the sort of thing that publishers want – something new to publish. The sexiest thing in publishing is always a new voice from somewhere new. That can become crude and bland, but if it's genuine, and I haven't heard from this part of the world much, then that's hugely exciting.

It's difficult for publishers to know where to go to find these new voices. Realistically, time is much better spent reading through what's already filtered through than encouraging people to write novels. The process is there not to exclude people – it's just the most efficient way.

Why don't publishers invest in mentors?
It's theoretically possible that publishers invest in mentors, though practically unlikely. Their margins are so small it's hard for them to make so abstract an investment.

In publishers' terms, does knowing a writer has been mentored carry any weight?
I might say, 'Good writers are bright people and it's great that this person has had the chance to work on their book with somebody clever.' Especially if I admire the writer who has mentored them.

Would you be more impressed by a writer having an MA in creative writing?
An MA in creative writing doesn't matter to me either way. I don't believe you can teach creative writing but you can give people time to learn. Time to write, focus to write, a forum to discuss. You can facilitate that group, make people comfortable, have insightful things to say. There is a danger that creative writing courses put out a product. In the 1990s you could pick up an American manuscript and tell which writing course it came out of. The good ones don't do that. If something comes from an agent I know and respect, that is more valuable to me than if it comes from a good writing programme.

How do you differentiate between an MA and mentoring?
An MA is just a formalised mentoring programme anyway. Mentoring is a kinder process for people fazed by the remoteness of academia. Its most valuable role is in reaching out a little more to people and saying that creative writing is not only for people who have been through Oxbridge. Zadie Smith was at Cambridge and Hari Kunzru was at Warwick, both journalists and plugged into that world, so they were always going to be ahead of the game in getting published. Mentors can reach places that publishers and agents can't.

Handling criticism
You are a writer engaged in a creative process that may well bring up difficult emotional material. You are quite likely to be sharing work in some embryonic stage, about which you are vulnerable. When you feel you have an issue with your mentor, pause for a while. Stay silent for a day or two. See if this period of silence lets you adjust and accept insights into your writing that were hard to take at first. If your mentor is good, you are likely to be gifted the occasional spell of such turmoil. It's part of the creative process. You may, of course, have ample reason to

be angry or disappointed with your mentor. You may also simply be projecting your creative struggle, fighting the mentor rather than yourself.

Therapists are trained to receive such projections of their patients' inner struggles. Writing mentors are not. They seek to focus on your writing. As writers they may be emotionally vulnerable themselves. One of the greatest fears of mentors is to be landed with a 'needy' mentee, constantly making demands on them. Remember that it is you who went looking for a mentor; the mentor did not come looking for you. Given that the mentor is less in need, being emotionally at some distance from your writing, is it possible that the difficulties in maintaining the relationship come from you? Are you, for example, taking comments personally rather than relating them to your craft?

The mentor may be lacking in certain social and educational skills that mean comments are delivered with less than ideal tact. If so, see if you can get over the manner of the delivery and focus on the comments themselves. Judge the relationship on its professional aspects.

You came in need of this professional relationship. The need may have been spurred by some sense of rejection from the world of publishing. Try to see the mentor more as a colleague than as an antagonist or competitor. If the relationship breaks down, it will simply bolster your sense of rejection. Go quiet. Take time. Think things through. Then communicate. Breakdown is a last resort. Keep things going if you can.

If you find criticism is more negative than you can easily handle, point this out. Ask the mentor to give you examples of what you are doing well. Positive feedback can be very helpful.

If you don't understand criticism, or don't know how to adapt your writing so as to deal with it, ask your mentor for help in doing so.

It's tempting to retaliate when criticised, to criticise in turn. Understand that any criticism is designed to help you with your work. When someone passes criticism of your work, an obvious and understandable reaction is to leap to its defence. Remember though, you don't need to accept someone's suggestion of *how* you should change something, even if that person is your mentor. You should, however, take the suggestion as some sort of marker in your text. This marker signals a point where a reader found some problem. You may not like that person's solution, but the need for some solution is evident. Go off and find your own! Your writing mentor is a respected reader as well as practitioner, and is highly likely to have much to offer your progress as a writer. The interactive nature of mentoring means your being active, doing your best to find out what the mentor is offering and then using it, however difficult the process might be.

Dealing with problems in the relationship

Don't hold the mentor to account for how your writing works out. Only you are responsible for that.

Should you feel the professional nature of your relationship has been violated in some way, perhaps you can work the problem out between you. Many problems can ultimately be ascribed to poor communication. So the first goal is to communicate.

You may also go to mediation. If a host organisation is involved, this is the point to check in with the person who brought you and the mentor together. The mediator may have other routes of communication or other information you are not party to.

For more serious issues, bringing in a mediator is the final option. The mentoring relationship is one of trust, and trust can seldom be mended once it is broken.

If things do break down, rather than worry about it, it's usually best to cut yourself loose – especially if you have set up the relationship yourself. The contract should state that in the event of a breakdown in the relationship both parties simply go their own way, and no more is owed in the way of mentoring or fees.

But remember, difficulties do not constitute a breakdown. Writing itself is 'difficult' – you can see even serious problems as learning experiences in themselves.

What does mentoring lead to?

How might a mentoring scheme prepare me for going it alone when it ends?

Mentoring is interactive, so you can make 'what do I do/where do I go next?' a question for your final session. If you reached your mentor through a literary organisation, contact the literature development officer there to see where they might direct you.

Hopefully, you will have learned enough from the mentoring period to take with you into a long, solitary run, shaping your work so that it reaches its full potential. It can be good to share your work, but it is also good to keep it wrapped up as your own gestating secret for a while.

What happens if I feel lonely?

We all know that, in the end, writing is a solitary and often lonely activity. You do not go into mentoring to make a friend (even if this is one thing that does happen) but to become a better writer. Now is the time to use what you have gained.

But you will be doing it from a new place: you should have renewed confidence in your own voice, your own potential. You should have new skills or understanding or ideas. You will have had the opportunity to spend time with someone who is already a 'professional' so you should have a stronger sense of what that might involve, and how to tackle the downsides of it all. You will have had the experience of a sustained period of solid writing work, with deadlines and direction. You may well find that, even if you do miss the sense of connection and the delight of having your work read and responded to sensitively, that the writer in you loves being alone to get on with it again.

None the less, some writers do discover that they need a peer group, contact with colleagues and a place to talk about writing seriously, in ways that can be very difficult with people who do not know much about the process. Some mentoring schemes encourage mentees to keep in touch with each other after the project has finished. If you get your mentoring through a scheme it is worth raising this with the managers, if they have not set it up already.

Can't I ask my mentor to carry on?

Of course you *can*. But the mentor may not want to and you may have difficulty getting more funding. In any case, mentoring is most effective in times of transition; you don't want to be in transition indefinitely.

Almost everyone we have spoken to who has had a good mentoring experience feels that they ended up ready and eager to carry on by themselves.

Trust the process.

For mentors

You're a writer with some significant success and experience behind you. Maybe you've worked as a mentor already, or maybe you're just wondering what such work might involve. This section is written for you.

What you're getting into

So tell me, what is a mentor?

You will find definitions elsewhere in this volume. Since this is the section of the book written for mentors, the answer here is 'you'. It may be worth peeling away a few layers to discover this 'you as mentor'. It can be helpful to see what role you *do* have by seeing what role you are *not* playing:

■ You are not an editor. You are not working toward a finished product, you are working to shift the writer to a new level.

■ You are not a copy editor. You don't need the writer to conform to a 'house style'. You don't need to deploy a gimlet eye for every mistake of grammar, punctuation or spelling.

■ You are not a teacher. Teachers have many virtues, but one vice you need to steer clear of is a tendency to establish a hierarchy in which 'teacher knows best'.

■ You are a mentor. That means you are a fellow writer. Your focus, unlike an editor or even a creative writing tutor, is on the writer not the product.

What's the difference between focusing on the product and on the writer?

It's fun if your mentee achieves professional success. The process remains dynamic so long as you can recognise some progress, some shift, in their work. But unlike an editor, you have nothing to gain from your writer's commercial success. Unlike a teacher, quantifiable results don't help you rise up a career ladder – mentoring has no such career structure.

Investing in your writer's commercial success is natural, but becoming too invested is a mistake. It means you are investing in the product not the work. Success or failure becomes measured by the publishing industry. In these terms, your true mentoring success, the strides your mentee went through as a writer, might be deemed a failure.

And if your writer is successful in the publishing world, it places her in direct competition with you. Your mentee is earning more than you are and gaining all the plaudits? Joy for the mentor in you, but potential agony for the writer.

Spare yourself. Focus on the writer not the product. Help that writer improve as much as you can.

What is a professional attitude to bring to mentoring?

The mentee has come to you as someone who is experienced and successful in the writing world. You've been through many of the doubts, the rejections, the trials of the business. You've learned from experience. You're somewhat calmer and less excited about the business aspect than you once were, and recognise some degree of mastery. You still have your own fears, your own concerns, your own emotions, but they need not interfere with your work as a mentor. A writer does not need to deal with the mentor's despair. You are as good a writer as you can be, and you want the same for your mentee. You are in a professional role, so you are friendly rather than being a friend.

Now a question for you. Who was your own mentor?

Think about it.

Your answer might be immediate and clear. If so, wonderful. You've had a blessing. But think again. Have you had a mentor in the way you are proposing becoming a mentor? The word 'mentor' is being used in a confusing number of ways. As we understand it, a mentor is not a 'role model'. A mentor must have engaged personally with you and your writing; a role model may well be dead, or at least someone you have never met.

Your answer might have been a friend. A relative. A writer friend. An editor. An agent. Was that person someone with a successful track record of negotiating the writing industry? Someone you did not know personally but whose work you respect? Someone who was paid to support your development as a writer? Was your relationship bound by contract and of an extended yet limited duration, with goals set out in advance? Was the focus on developing you as a writer rather than on preparing a piece of work for publication? Was it exclusively on a one-to-one basis?

If the answer to all of those points is yes, then you have had a mentor as understood by the writers of this book. However, mentoring in this professional way is still quite new. There are few second-generation mentors: those who have been through a mentorship and are now sufficiently established in their trade to mentor others.

So it is quite likely you did not have a mentor, at least in the way you are now thinking about for yourself. That means you have not had a clear professional model. In becoming a mentor, it's interesting to see how you are becoming the mentor you would have liked in your life all those years ago. You know a lot about being an emerging writer, because you have been one yourself. Become the mentor you would like to have had.

A game to play

Step back in time. From among the pantheon of writers in the past, whom would you like to have had as a mentor? Why that particular writer? Imagine how they might have entered your writing process. What direction might your writing have taken? What years of trial and error could they have helped you speed across? What fun would it have been?

You can take the same degree of imagination into imagining yourself as a mentor.

A follow-up game

Whom would you like as a mentor now?

This helps you see that the mentor/mentee relationship is actually two writers working together, one simply more experienced than the other.

You have become very good at what you do. You are an expert. Yet maybe there is still somebody in your chosen field from whom you think you could learn. We all learn all the time, with every new project we embark upon.

Or maybe there is some other area of writing that appeals to you, which you have never fully tackled. Perhaps you're a poet who would like to try fiction; a novelist who is interested in a shift towards biography; a short story writer who would like to write dramatic monologues. Mentoring can work well across forms. We can all learn from others. Being a mentor doesn't stop you becoming a mentee as well some day.

What's in it for you?

Does it pay?

This book is setting out the professional code for mentoring. That means you get paid.

If you are part of a scheme, the organising institution will have its own system of payment.

If you are working it out for yourself, estimate what your rate of pay is for a day's work: that is a fair rate to charge for a mentoring session. A full day's pay should cover all the administration involved in arranging the meeting; the time reading and re-reading the submitted manuscript; the time preparing your critique; and the time spent travelling.

Freelance writing can mean pulling in sums from many different areas. Mentoring can offer a significant strand of income.

If you have never thought about your time in this sort of way you can get up-to-date advice on where to go for guidance on appropriate pay rates from your Arts Council England literature officer. Bear in mind that you are trying to help your mentees become more 'professional' – offering them less than professional rates not only undermines you, it undermines them and other writers too.

Isn't there a history of successful writers helping those starting out, without getting paid for it?

There is. But the writers you are thinking of were lucky – they already knew other writers prepared to mentor them. Now professional mentoring has an outreach quality, putting successful writers together with those who would not normally have access to them. Professional mentoring is quite new on the creative writing scene. Should you simply want to mentor as part of your sense of service to society, without pay, this book should still help you do so at a professional level.

How do I get paid?

If you are applying to some organised scheme, the organisation will deal with this. If not, our suggestion is that you are paid for each session, at the beginning of the session. In that way, should the relationship break down in any way, the financial aspects of the dissolution should not be too messy. The important thing in a 'private' mentoring relationship is to discuss and agree the details at the outset. If your writer has received a grant to pay you, for example from Arts

Council England, it may be a good idea to ask them to put the money in a separate account.

What's the maximum number of mentees I can take on at any one time?

This varies. Three can be comfortable, one can be fine. Some mentors work with six or more. However, if you're mentoring for financial reasons alone, it might be worth looking for some form of financial support to get your own writing back on track. Mentoring works best when it augments your writing rather than replaces it.

How might being a mentor help my own writing?

It's hard to be wholly subjective about one's own work. Giving close attention to someone else's work, having to offer a constructive critique rather than a judgment, often results in your articulating perceptions that you can then apply to your own work.

Writing is often a lonely and undervalued profession. Many people respond to meeting writers by saying, "I've got a book I want to write some day" as though writing is something you can coast into once your real business is done. Mentees, however, should bring due regard if not awe for all you have achieved: respect can be encouraging. Simply having to be upfront about all the skills you have acquired in your professional life can be empowering. Mentoring can make you aware of your own skills. Your subsequent writing may stem from renewed self-confidence.

Some mentors find their ideal readers in their mentees. They feel no one has ever read them so acutely before, not simply seeking entertainment or looking to judge, but working to discover and appreciate all those writerly aspects you infused into the work. Too often we don't realise our own strengths. Just as it is part of your job as a mentor to point out the mentees' strengths, so you can gain from having your own noted.

When you mentor, you are entering into a dialogue with another writer, and who knows what might spring from that? Mentoring beyond your known safety range, – say to someone of a different age, background, gender, race, location, social perspective, writing agenda, sexuality, audience, or attitude to your own – can wake you to fresh possibilities. Suddenly your mentee offers you glimpses of something different and this may alert you to creative opportunities you have so far ignored.

Writers find material in the 'real world'. Your mentee becomes a vital aspect of that real world. It is unlikely that your writing won't develop as a result.

How might being a mentor harm my own writing?

To be a mentor, you must have achieved some professional standing. You should have a fair degree of confidence in your own writing, and mentoring should have no adverse affect.

Some writers need to be reclusive when writing. In the white heat of creativity it might not suit you to have to break from your own work to consider someone else's. You can choose not to mentor during such periods, or negotiate a break.

Mentoring is a real responsibility. One possible danger is that you become more engrossed in your mentee's creative process than in your own. You can prevent that by being very professional about how much time you give to the project. Since writers do have a tendency to give their time away for free, you may have to work on this. If your imagination does get too caught up in a mentee's project, work out why it has excited you so much. See if you can apply what you have learned to your own work.

Another danger is that you mentor too much. Mentoring is a complement to writing, not a replacement for it. Mentoring can harm your writing if it takes too much time away from it.

You may dislike your mentee's writing to the point of its being dispiriting. Since you should have liked a sample of her writing before taking her on, you can bring this up for discussion. See if you can get the mentee back on the track you liked. If you can't, be positive and find *something* to like, or you won't be able to mentor effectively. Work it out, or cut your losses and move on.

You need to keep the focus on the mentee's writing, not her life. If the relationship becomes emotional it will take up more of your life than is its due. That might harm your writing.

Your mentee may become 'the next young thing', bounding with enthusiasm, have agents and publishers in hot pursuit, while your own *magnum opus* is ignored. Never mind. Stifle envy. Accept a sliver of credit. Remember all those ups and downs of your own professional life and be glad for someone else's highs. Success is delicate and transitory and worth celebrating. Keep even keel. Who knows, your mentee might be in a position to give your work support one day and help it on its way.

Mentoring should not harm your writing at all, and is likely to enhance it. Making mistakes in mentoring might affect you though.

How do I know if the emerging writer and I will get on?

Consider a sample of their writing first. See if it engages and excites you in some way. You need to feel good about the writing, and to sense that you can help sharpen it or move it into some new dimension.

I'd be happy to mentor but am shy of commitment in all areas of my life apart from writing. Any advice?

Mentoring is a commitment. Start small – one writer for one fixed period of time may not be beyond you. If you feel comfortable with that, try it out and see what happens. Alternatively, apply to be a mentor for an organisation offering mentoring schemes; in this context you will have some affirmation in being selected, and some support from the project management. If either or both of these suggestions still seem like too much commitment, you need to ask yourself what the 'happy' in your question might actually mean. As a mentor you are the strongest element in the partnership and should not be in need of too much hand-holding from anyone else.

Setting yourself up as a mentor

How successful do I need to be, in terms of publications, to become a mentor?

Essentially, you need to be more successful in your chosen field than your mentee is. You might of course be largely unpublished yet potentially brilliant as a mentor: if years of learning your craft have given you confidence, you might well be ready to mentor.

Usually however, you would bring some publication record along with you. That's largely how the world-at-large can judge you. A story or poem in a prominent journal may be enough. If you're in doubt, it may be best to turn to the first section of this book and see whether a period of being a mentee might be what's best for you. A mentee may well be a writer with some real success, looking to step up a level.

Does mentoring need a sponsoring body, or can I set up in business independently?

Stay tuned to developments, because one aim of this book is that more organisations will consider funding mentoring schemes for creative writers. It could well be worth registering your interest in mentoring with your local literature or theatre officer, so that you can be matched with any suitable mentee who might approach them. Recently, Arts Council England has given bursary funding to emerging writers, with a specific mentoring element attached; usually, successful applications of this kind have been made with the proposed mentor already on board. If you have a writer whom you would like to work with, it might be sensible to submit a joint application or support the writer through the application process. Among other advantages, this makes the whole process of agreeing your fees more transparent and less personal.

We believe that in the next few years there is likely to be a real growth in commercial agencies offering mentoring. Such agencies already exist in a small way. You can apply to them for work. Although you will be less well paid working in this way rather than independently, as the organisations will need to cover their overheads, there are real benefits, especially when you are just starting; they will provide you with clients, mediate if things go awry and handle all the administration for you. The normal model here is for the organisation (rather than the mentee) to be the employer, and you may feel more comfortable this way rather than working directly with your mentee as your 'boss'.

Individual writers have set themselves up as small businesses, marketed largely on the internet, offering mentoring services. It would make sense for writers to team up in offering such services, so that a suitable match between mentor and mentee could be drawn from a larger pool of talent.

I'd like to help writers from disadvantaged communities. Are grants available?

The short answer is, yes, there are. However, there are some issues here, which you need to be clear about. If you think of writers from socially excluded communities as *disadvantaged* there are going to be problems! The writing community (including publishers, as Ben Ball made clear in the previous chapter) is keen to find new voices and where members of minority communities can bridge the skills gap and gain access, there is a case for suggesting they are distinctly *advantaged.*

One of the problems for socially marginalised communities is low aspirations. Here, role models – members of those communities who have established themselves as writers – may be particularly valuable as mentors. However, both of the authors of this book worked on Crossing Borders, which delivered online mentoring to emerging African writers. In most of the countries where the project ran, the writers were disadvantaged by an inadequate infrastructure, not by low aspirations or shortage of role models, and where the mentors were sensitive to cultural difference, the project worked extremely well.

It is also true that various organisations are becoming increasingly aware of the possibilities of reaching their goals through the creative arts, even when those goals are not overtly literary. Mentoring life-writing in the hospice movement, for example, might offer invaluable support for the dying and their friends and relatives. Mentoring might empower members of communities who don't currently see their lives, needs and aspirations reflected in the media. Mentoring by distance-learning can reach people in remote regions, or those with access issues, who are otherwise marginalised.

Mentoring differs from community arts projects because, by definition, it is directed at the individual writer rather than at a community or group. If you are looking to help a disadvantaged community rather than work with a talented writer, mentoring creative writing may not be the most effective way to use your time.

With all that stated, there is a whole host of excellent reasons why authorities might well offer grants to writing mentors. Be creative. Come up with those reasons, and go for it. A practical starting point might be to approach those communities, through their own organisations, or approach your local literature development officer and talk through what you might see yourself doing in the field.

Can I mentor out of my own language?

This isn't usual, but the question is included to allow for speakers of minority languages who wish to write in that language but have no available mentors. You might help with translations of poetry into English, for example. A novelist in a minority language may very likely wish her work to stand comparison with novels of any language. While choosing to write in her own language, she may gain a great deal from the chance to debate her choices of character, narrative techniques, use of dialogue etc with a novelist who works in a majority language. The nature of the meetings might be less formal, less focused on text, but a sequence of programmed chats over coffee with someone experienced in waging the writer's life might well help break what might otherwise feel like unhelpful isolation.

Or suppose English is not your mother tongue. Mentoring – even with a writer who does not speak your own language – can still be valuable. Ignatius Mabasa, a Zimbabwean poet and novelist who writes in Shona as well as English, told us:

"For myself, I'm interested in supporting writing in minority languages and cross-language mentoring. The Shona novel has failed to develop. Shona parents speak to their children in English. There are no possible mentors. Most writers write from the head, transferring techniques found in other literatures (eg, *King Lear* in Shona is one of the major novels, drawn directly from the Shakespeare play), and not from the heart. It is possible to mentor from one language to another, given the context – eg, discussion of plot, character, place etc."

Negotiating your contract

If you are part of an organised scheme it will likely present its own contract. Otherwise we offer a sample Mentoring Agreement at the end of this book. Mentorship is a process of agreement through negotiation, so you can use our Agreement as a starting point. Fill in the blanks as suits you both, and feel free to strike any clauses that do not fit your circumstances or add any you feel are necessary.

Do I have to sign a contract, or can I keep things informal?

The Mentoring Agreement we suggest is not very restrictive (see Appendix 1) and helps both sides understand what is involved. Since you are starting a professional relationship, a contract makes good sense. But if both you and your mentee agree to do without one for some reason, then that serves as its own form of contract and you both choose to run with any liabilities that may incur. However, if you do not have a contract you will have to issue individual invoices for each payment to keep the tax office contented and off your back.

While you do not *have* to have a contract, we would very strongly recommend that you do.

Is it OK to have a rolling relationship rather than a fixed-term one, keeping it going so long as it feels good for both sides?

A fixed term is useful, so that the mentoring stays positive and does not just peter out. It saves embarrassment too – it allows each party a moment at which they can end the relationship without criticism of the other. You also do not want to encourage dependency. The mentee should fledge at some point.

One alternative is to mentor through the duration of a project – a cycle of poems, for example; a play; the first draft of a novel.

There is, after all, nothing to stop you both entering into a new contract at the end of the initial period if that feels right.

Getting down to work

The first meeting: setting the goals

If you have not already met your writer, do so! (Or if you are working on distance mentoring, write to them.) This first meeting should establish your mode for punctuality, and be kept to the agreed duration. The main purpose of this first meeting is to get to know each other a little and also to arrange a timetable and set the goals.

However *the most important thing* to do if you have not had an opportunity to do so before, and even if you have, is to respond positively to the writing you should have seen already. Be specific – pick something in the sample writing, or from the writer's past work, that you genuinely like. Try to give them some sense of what it is in their writing that excites you, and why you have taken this work on. If you cannot do this sincerely then you should not enter into a contract with this individual.

The mentee may have set some goals in meeting the manager of your scheme, if you are part of one. Perhaps she set out some goals in her initial application. Possibly some goals came in notes accompanying her first submitted piece.

For your part, you have read the writing sample, based on which you reached your decision to work with this mentee. And now you have read and prepared a session from your notes.

This first time around, before taking the steps sketched out in 'The session' section later in this book, it's a good idea to focus on the bigger picture. Don't go straight to the submitted text. Instead try a question such as: 'What sort of writer do you think of yourself as being?' 'What would you say are your main strengths as a writer?' 'What excites you most about the way you write?'

You have some ideas of your own from what you've read. Through discussion, see how your sense of the mentee as a writer fits in with her own. You might then ask the question, 'What do you want to take away with you from this whole mentorship?'

Reserve some time at the end of your session in which to set goals. That stops the session from drifting. Move on to considering the writing so your mentee has more of a sense of what mentoring actually is. You can both then bring observations gained from the writing sample into setting those goals. One big goal or a few precise ones may be enough.

In forming realistic goals, the experience of the mentor has to be actively brought into play. Even if the mentee comes to you with a list of six goals, you will still have to engage with that. The goals should always be informed by your input. See more about this in the section of this book for mentees and emerging writers.

This meeting is also an opportunity to make sure that you both have a shared understanding of how and when (and if) you can be contacted outside the arranged sessions.

At the end of this meeting you need to have a date, time and place fixed for the first full session. You will probably want to suggest accurately what you expect to see, with an emphasis on new writing, and how long in advance of the meeting you need to receive it.

Preparing for your sessions

Working on the submitted manuscript

Ideally, the piece that has been submitted is accompanied by the mentee's notes. This commentary should be a required element of distance learning work. Even prior to face-to-face meetings, some notes from the mentee are truly helpful. Approaching an agent or an editor, the writer's work is required to stand on its own. The writer needs to put on a brave face and sound positive. With a mentor the writer can afford to be self-analytical and vulnerable. We'll consider the mentee's commentary or notes later.

The models we offer in this section are personal, reflecting the authors' own practice. If you mentor already, it might offer some variety to your own model. If not, it's a tried and tested place to start.

Step one

Read the piece *as a reader*. Maybe have a pencil to hand. What you are doing this first time is noting your gut responses. Your notes may simply be a tick or a cross in the margin, marking the places that triggered positive or negative reactions.

Some places to tick?
- Your attention is gripped.
- The language excites you.
- Some shift in tone or content rouses you.

Some places to cross?
- Your attention has wandered.
- You've had to step back in your reading to make sense of things.
- You're brought up by some inconsistency or contradiction.
- The language draws too much attention to itself.

Step two

You now have your informed reader's response. At this point your 'like/dislike' opinion is possibly in place. And you may have early questions you would like to ask the writer.

This is a good time to shift from the piece of writing to any accompanying notes or commentary. Some mentors prefer to read such notes before the work itself. This can be fine if it's what you prefer. Saving the commentary till 'step two' does mean, however, that the piece of work has had one 'virgin' read. The writing has stood alone for a while, and has had to speak for itself.

Step three
You may choose to jump right over this step. Some mentors prefer to work in a white heat, a concentrated burst of the necessary hours of reading and written response. For those who choose it, though, 'Step three' is time out. Let the reading gather inside yourself as you move on through some of the other items in your day. Even a quick break to put on the kettle can be helpful at this point.

Step four
You have read the work once, and considered any accompanying notes. This second reading is different. You have moved on from being the 'informed reader' to being the writer at work. Your job this time is to elucidate those ticks and crosses, to articulate the reasons behind your visceral reactions.

Step five
You have now read the piece twice. The second reading was slower than the first, and probably involved reading different sections a number of times. 'Step five' is 'preparing your act'. Maybe one more reading does the job. The job, 'your act', is knowing what you want to accomplish with the writer, knowing how to do so, and having your notes arranged accordingly.

The better, the more highly polished, the piece of work is, the more times you may have to read it. Your job is to move the writer to the next stage. If what you are presented with seems publishable as it is, you have to really raise your game. It's good to spend time pointing out why a piece is so good, but always interesting to offer some way that it might be developed further.

If the writing contains many areas which might be improved, just this one more reading should do the job. You have no shortage of material for your session, so now just need to select and marshal it.

The manuscript submitted by your mentee has entered a creative process. For now, you are transforming it into your 'script' that you will use for your session together with the mentee. This script provides you with all of your prompts. If you are working in distance learning mode, your commentary will take the place of a face-to-face session. This same preparation of a script will set you up for writing your commentary.

The mentee's manuscript as your 'script':

■ You may want some coloured markers or pencils to hand.

■ Each session is part of a programme. Prioritise. You don't have to deal with everything at once. Let some things go and choose a focus for the session. This might stem from those visceral reactions, the things that really gave you a problem as a reader. One major area to work on might be enough. Perhaps add a couple of other, simpler issues that are easier for the mentee to work on. Examples of a major area: the introduction of new characters or the use of descriptive detail. Simpler areas: repetition of words, or confusion in the use of tenses.

■ Ultimately you will be handing these notes on to your mentee. Don't worry about this too much for now. But do you remember times when the proofs of your beautiful work came back from a copy editor, larded with corrections you found largely irritating and irrelevant? It's disheartening to find your manuscript choked with points to correct. Don't overdo it.

■ Take your coloured markers, one colour for each issue, and mark the manuscript where these issues arise.

■ Also take a pencil and mark in the margin those sections of the manuscript that you would like to scrutinise alongside your mentee. These are short areas that seem awkward to you in some way.

■ Take a different colour – maybe gold, or one of those 'smiley' stamps! – and mark sections in the manuscript that are ripe for praise. Think of yourself as a writer. Remember how stimulating praise can be, and how rare. We often need to be shown what we do particularly well.

Step six

This one's optional. However if you can rise to it, it's worth doing.

What other writers did your mentee's writing put you in mind of? Note them down. Just as your writing career is more advanced than your mentee's, the scope of your reading is something you can draw on for the mentee's benefit. We all learn from the writing of others. Suggest appropriate reading for the mentee. You might even take a copy along with you, so as to share a few lines. A lot might be gained from discussing the work of someone else.

That's it. You're fully prepared. Time for the session.

NB: Those who are to be working in distance learning mode will now move on to writing their commentary. You might consider writing such a commentary even if your session with the mentee will be 'face-to-face'.

Reasons you might do this:
■ It's your first meeting and you like the confidence of knowing you are well prepared. As a writer, you are more comfortable displaying your strengths in text than in a more improvised, spoken way.
■ This written commentary provides a truly useful written record of response and instruction, which the mentee can refer back to through the months ahead.
■ You want to keep to your schedule of meetings but life has called you or your mentee to some other part of the planet. Interspersing a session in distance learning mode can be a useful variant to your usual meetings, and keep you on schedule.
■ Equal exchange, getting away from any 'teacher' aspect. You have a document of the writer's, and now they have a document of yours.

One obvious reason for not doing it: It takes up time for which you are not necessarily being paid. Time is precious. The written commentary takes the place of a face-to-face session and is not supposed to supplement it.

The commentary might address these kinds of comments:
■ What caused your attention to wander?
■ Why did you have to pause and go back?
■ Why did a piece of the writing stand out in the way it did?
■ If it stands out as being especially good, what made it so? Does the rhythm of the preceding lines help make it stand out, or does it stand out in contrast to less effective writing?
■ If it stands out as being especially weak, what makes it so? If it's cliché, mark it as such. If a line seems especially tortured, if it's overweighted with clauses, if its adverbs seem particularly noisome, mark it as such.
■ You're not editing the piece. You're making notes of where the writer needs to pay particular attention. These are your notes as much as the writer's. These are the platforms from which your session with the writer will spring.

The sessions

This is a suggested pattern for a regular, face-to-face session. Skip steps, juggle the order, add new items to suit your situation. This is simply a model that works. Change it as you see fit, or come back to it should things be going astray.

Remember that each session with the mentee is one session, one part of a much larger and sustained programme. You don't need to nail everything down. It's helpful at this point to remember all those roles you are *not* playing – editor, copy editor, teacher, friend etc.

Settling in

You should both have a copy of the text. Yours is your 'script', the manuscript you have read and annotated. Your mentee's is probably clean. That way she can focus on the writing without worrying about interpreting your comments and markings. It's good for you both to have text you can look at. It's hard to maintain eye contact all the time in a one-on-one situation. It's better at such moments to look at the text rather than around the room. Also, you are talking about your mentee's writing. She's vulnerable and you should bear this in mind.

Once you are both settled, note the time. Keeping to your time limit is a good way of showing yourself to be a professional. You know as well as anyone that 'outsiders' tend to place little value on a writer's time. They wonder how you get away with not having a proper job. Your mentee is a fellow writer. If she doesn't yet know how precious a writer's time is, now is a good time to show her.

Your mentee is waiting. You're in the role of expert. They have sent you their work. You have read it. So... what do you think? They're desperate for a verdict. It's natural. You've got an hour or so to deliver the whole truth. Start with some encouragement. 'This was terrific. I loved it,' should go down fine. If that's not true, you can come up with something. 'This had real energy.' 'This was a really brave piece.' 'It was raw, but the passion really came through.' 'I've never read anything like it. It's really out there.'

Listen for the response. It's likely to be along the lines of: "What a relief. I thought you'd hate the part where..." As soon as you have triggered a response, you have a dialogue. This isn't the moment to backtrack and start condemning the piece. You're being friendly.

Stay general before getting specific. Try out another opening question, such as 'What was your biggest challenge in this piece?' 'How easily

did this piece flow?' 'What was the part you worked on hardest?'
'How is this piece different?' This is a good time to refer to any notes
the writer provided alongside the piece, and enter discussion on them.
It's also a time in which you could allow the writer to bring up any
writing concern of her own, or any specific questions she would like you
to address.

Offer a section you have marked as being particularly effective. Maybe
read it aloud. *Ask* your writer why you might think it's so good. This
works better than *telling* the writer why you think the piece works.
She's on safe ground. She knows you like it. She has nothing to defend.
She starts to voice a critique of her own work. Recognising what's good
about our own work is one of the chief skills a writer has to learn.
Imagine having to tell someone why you're so good. It's a healing thing
to do, and gives confidence. If you have anything left to say after your
writer has spoken, then say it.

Select one of those passages that you have some questions about.
Ask your writer to read that section aloud from her own copy. Then ask
her to comment on it. Reading one's own work aloud is a good
technique. It slows one down and helps one hear things for the first
time. If you found something awkward in the writing, hopefully your
writer will sense the same awkwardness and be able to say what
causes it. There's just a chance that a line that you want to challenge is
the writer's favourite line. If you think it's rubbish, now is the time to say
so and why. You won't always agree and don't have to, so long as you
can both explain yourselves.

Explain that you have three (or however many) areas that you want to
look at together. From now on you can both focus on your 'script'.
Work through your colour codings so that the issues are dealt with one
at a time.

Introduce your 'big issue'. Your main focus is building on strengths
rather than highlighting weaknesses. Don't try to bring things into the
writing that don't so far exist. If you want to work on the rhythm of
particular lines, find somewhere in the writing where rhythm is deployed
effectively. If it's not possible to find such an example, then the writer is
not yet ripe for developing the rhythm in her writing. Similarly if you think
the piece might gain from more descriptive detail, find somewhere in the
piece where some such detail appeared.

Work through one instance where the writing might be developed
along the lines you are suggesting.

Leave your writer to consider an extra example on her own, marking
any changes onto the script. Stay quiet while she does so. When she's
ready, consider and discuss the change. Move on when you both sense
some real advance is made. If that sense of advance doesn't come fairly

quickly, move on in any case. You only have a limited time and don't need to get bogged down on one point.

Come across one or two of those points you've highlighted that are worthy of praise. Take time to offer that praise and say why something is so good.

Move on to your other, smaller areas for consideration. A good technique is often to ask your writer to cut a word or a line. Work can often be improved by cutting. Another good trick is pointing out one of the areas you have marked for change without saying what the change might be. See if your writer can work it out for herself, and make the change.

Take time to discuss what you both think are the real strengths in the piece of work.

Scan through your 'script' together. It is about to become the mentee's record of your meeting. She will take it away and burrow through it, seeking a firmer grasp on how to apply what you say to how she writes. She may well come back to it a year from now, when memories of the meeting have faded to nothing. Take time to make sure the mentee understands all your notes, and write clarifications where necessary. Your notes are likely to be less tactful than you have been during the session. If anything strikes you as harsh, take time to explain it. Hand over the notes.

Have the writer say in what way she might develop her writing. Give her time to take notes of this.

Do you want to suggest any challenges for the next submission? If you want to see something in the writer's work that has yet to make an appearance — for example dialogue, or use of the second person voice – introduce the idea now. Say why it might be effective. Talk through any perceived difficulties. Ask her to try it out for next time.

Check the writer feels OK about the session. Deal with any concerns.

What are you both reading? What reading recommendations can you give? What's the state of your own writing life just now? Use the rest of your allotted slot for some writers' downtime. End the session as relaxed fellow writers about to move on.

Some variations to consider

Using a laptop

One of you might bring the text on a laptop. Sometimes it is interesting to look at different ways the work might appear on a page.

Poetry is the most obvious candidate for concern about how the work is presented on the page. It is a more obviously visual medium. Poets might be encouraged to see how breaks of lines and stanzas could reflect their own vocal delivery of a poem. They might have fun seeing how dialect works on a page. They can try dividing a poem according to rhythm, according to emotion, or according to sense, so as to understand what variants might come into play. They could see how the shape of a poem might reflect its content. Font choices might become elements of the visual experience of a poem.

Working in prose, paragraphing skills is a good area to look at in this way. A piece might be visually dense and therefore unnecessarily daunting. Some writers and readers are thrilled by a page dense with text. On a laptop, two options could be displayed for a writer to compare.

If you are focusing on the skill of editing a piece down, a laptop can come in handy. Single words might go, or perhaps when your talk focuses on what a prose piece is truly about and what might be extraneous to it, whole paragraphs or pages may vanish. This can be done on paper, but the end result can look like a massacre and be spread over page after page. Working in the 'track changes' mode in Microsoft Word, you could suddenly hide all those changes and clean text emerges. Instead of a massacre you are looking at a gem.

Some mentors prefer to work on screen rather than paper. For them, notions of deploying coloured crayons, marker pens, pencils and smiley stamps will seem quaint and antiquated. It's clearly possible to have your 'script', fully annotated and colour coded, as a file on your computer and work from that. You could write additional comments during the session and review the pages together in the same way as you might on paper. You then even have a chance to review your script before emailing it on to your mentee after your session together, including any thoughts that might have cropped up in the meantime. You might both be surfing some wireless-enabled technological wave that bursts beyond the bounds of this book. If so, enjoy it and let us know how you got on!

Presentation of manuscripts to professional standard

The publishing industry requires material to be presented in standard ways. If the piece you are working on falls short of those standards, it makes sense to address them on screen. Rather than simply speak of the needs for double spacing, for margins, for indentations, for page numbering, it is more effective to guide the mentee through the relevant keystrokes to bring the changes about. Seeing the correct model appear on the screen is a valuable and memorable experience.

The computer as a writer's tool

In what ways does a computer support your writing?

Simply zooming out to 25%, so a long piece of writing has its pages tiled upon your screen, can be helpful in terms of understanding the layout of a piece, for example – and for getting some visual understanding of the volume of your achievement. It's a trick you might share.

As you're writing, note any personal quirks in the way you use your computer – and see if these might be worth passing on.

You might also give brief demonstrations of any software packages you use. If your mentee is a screenwriter, introducing her to the Final Draft screenwriting programme might open up a whole world of possibilities.

The computer as research tool

If you are mentoring a biographer, or a life-writer, you might give guidance on how to use different search engines and search terms. You might also direct some quest through the pages of national archives, museums or libraries.

As a poet, what have you bookmarked as favourite sites? You might share these, and consider how your mentee might find an online audience for her work.

Make it interactive

There may well be a generational divide between mentor and mentee. At all points, accept that your mentee might have something to teach you. Don't be afraid to pick up skills from your mentee. If pen and paper has always been grand for you and you see no reason to change now, fair enough. You can even have a go at persuading your mentee of the advantages of stepping back in time. But you shouldn't require it. We don't need our mentees to become like us. We want them to be the most exciting and complete version of themselves, whatever it takes.

Punctuation as breath

You are not a copy editor, required to correct all your mentee's punctuation. However, it can be worth taking a little time to talk it through. You might copy-edit a short section, and show how those corrections need applying throughout a writer's work. The lack of effective punctuation may just come from never having had punctuation explained.

Also, if your mentee cannot punctuate, it is hard to move on to discovering the appropriate rhythm in a sentence – especially in prose.

You might read a sentence as it is punctuated. Have the mentee read a sentence aloud and see where she pauses, where the voice rises or falls. Simple rules such as a comma for a short pause, a full stop for a long one, and that the voice tends to rise before a comma and drop before a full stop, can help. Essentially, letters are the way that sound is marked on paper, and punctuation is the way that breath is marked on paper. It is good to show writers how they can link words so that they lead towards a silence for the reader, in which those words can take effect. One step of being able to write towards a silence is being allowed to punctuate. If you can help in this, feel free to do so.

Hot-seating

Sometimes you want to shift a mentee's work into a new dimension. Leaving the text in favour of conversation might be a way of facilitating this.

Perhaps a piece of writing stems from your writer's own experience. The writing might be blocked because the writer has not achieved a sufficient distance from the material. Simply asking, 'Where does this piece stem from?' might bring out some information. Your aim is not, quite definitely not, to tromp around in your writer's psyche. You are not an analyst. But you might be able to offer techniques, 'tricks of the trade', that allow a writer to haul her writing over a particular blockage and move it on. For instance, it's often helpful to take some aspect of a remembered situation and change it in some way. If someone was short in real life, make them tall. Make a thin person fat. A calm person liable to fits of temper. Change someone's gender or age. Relocate a situation to somewhere entirely different. Changing some aspect of remembered reality like that can be like pressing a lever, so that the power of fiction flows through.

A powerful game you can play for five or ten minutes is to 'hot-seat' your writer. Have them assume the role of a character in their fiction, and answer your questions as that character. Surprise them with your questions, such as 'What was your first memory?' 'What are your table manners like?' 'Who don't you trust in your life?' Answering such questions immerses a writer in her own story, and often leads to new developments.

Similarly you could place a poet inside the landscape of a poem and ask questions about it. 'What's the most exciting thing achieved by light in this place?' 'How would you like to change this place?' 'What's the coolest spot to sit in?' 'Does it always smell the same?'

Novelist Jill Dawson offers her own reflections on being a mentor:
"As a mentor, relationships always surprise me. I start off being hesitant, even though I liked the work enough to take it on. By the second session it *is* about sharing all I know in the world – writing. The only person to really value that is someone who writes. To share all of that, to see someone grappling with all of that, is morale boosting.

"When talking with students to set their goals, it is good to steer them away from final product. So if a mentee says, 'I want to get a novel published', suggest instead, 'I want to write the best novel I can.' If they want a full critique, I may give them a full critique of one page, but explain the advantages of working in other ways.

"I start each meeting by thanking the mentee for what they have sent, and say how much I loved or liked it. I don't lie, but I always find some positive to start from. As a writer I find that silence is terrifying. If I give someone my book and don't hear back from them I know there may be many reasons for this, but always presume it's because they did not like it. When mentees come into a meeting they are filled with wanting to hear what you thought about their work. Starting with encouragement normally brings out their own anxieties, eg, 'I thought you would hate it because...' So it's a good basis for starting a discussion.

"I tend to be firm, setting deadlines and word limits. Being apparently firm allows a lot of safety. Time is massively precious. Let people see that writing time is precious to you. Part of what mentees get from the mentor is seeing how writers actually finish books. In the meetings I keep the conversation on the writing. This is valuable time which needs using well. When mentees try and lead the conversation into other fields it is generally a sign of their insecurity with the process of speaking about their own writing, or perhaps they are uncomfortable with the nature of their material. Because mentees do email and contact each other, it is important that mentors stick to the contracted hours and don't overrun them. If one mentor does so, the pressure is there for others to follow suit or for mentees to be disappointed.

"Some mentees say, 'It's different for you because you're published.' That's not so. I've always applied deadlines of my own and imposed measures of self-discipline.

"I like to work out issues in my own writing, not in other people's work. However, being a mentor does make me better as a writer – being diligent about the mentees' writing helps me apply that diligence to my own.

"It's important to keep some informality about the process. My current mentee suddenly found herself pregnant in her forties. It was possible to be flexible about the schedule of support, and this allows her to believe her novel is not scuppered because she is having a baby.

"I spend time telling people what it is they are doing right. I am tactful in the meeting but not so tactful in my notes, where I may just have written 'Nonsense'. I take time to explain my notes. I always make sure that I place lots of positives in the notes, praising what is good, and find that is very effective in bringing about results.

"I don't rewrite work – I am aware of mentees' fears of mentors with their greater experience and reputation imposing their voice on the writing. I may sometimes take out words and show in that way how taking out words can make a sentence beautiful.

"When I started out as a writer I was envious of those with writers in their families, where writing was seen as normal, belonging to a circle, being able to show your work to someone who was published. That's one reason I feel so passionate about mentoring, providing the thing I never had but always wanted – access to people to whom writing *really* matters."

Distance learning

The delivery

Distance learning is a highly viable alternative to a face-to-face session, with some built-in bonuses. Yet it has to work extra hard to deliver the personal side: usually through tone of voice, through gesture, through a smile, through a silence.

Mentoring works best through an interactive relationship. It involves the mentor listening as much as speaking. Somehow, within the narrative of your own critique, you need to encompass much of the personality of the relationship. In conversation, you know how your comments are being received and can adjust accordingly. In written communication, you cannot adjust what you have said in order to get the appropriate response. You need to be aware that words on paper can be read in many different ways, and work to safeguard your actual intention.

Distance learning leaves the mentor prone to 'delivering' a tutorial. In itself this can be fine. You are the expert and have a lot to deliver. Your particular expertise is in writing, so what better mode to 'deliver' in than the written word. You can take your time to achieve a sustained narrative that makes sense and builds towards the appropriate conclusion. Your mentee will gain simply from close engagement with you as a writer, in your chosen medium. Lucky them – they have an experienced writer who has agreed to write about their writing.

The main chance for added interactivity comes with the mentee's accompanying notes, what we will call a commentary. This is where your writer can voice her concerns. Where does this piece of writing stem from in her life? How does it fit into the context of her other writings? What were her hopes for it when she started out? How well have these hopes been realised? What was the biggest challenge? What's the biggest success and the most significant failure? Has she used any other writer as a model? Does she think it starts or ends well? Was this piece written slowly? Was it rushed?

Sometimes it is hard to squeeze this information out of the mentee. Think about why. As a writer, especially when you were starting out, how many people had patience for such rumination about your art? You now not only have patience, but you have an informed interest. Your mentee has very likely never had anyone like you in her life. So be encouraging. Let her know that you not only want to hear her thoughts about her work, but that such thoughts are vital.

Is this true? Do you have to hear what your mentee thinks about her writing? Can't you just work from the writing itself?

Of course you can. But if you do, it's hard to distinguish between your role and that of an editor. The collegiate side of mentoring, the 'fellow writers in it together' aspect, is hard to sustain. Remember that this written tutorial replaces the face-to-face session. Imagine turning up to that face-to-face, giving it your all for an hour, going away again, yet in all that time your mentee never got to utter a sentence. Your writer's commentary is the one chance you get to listen. Work at it, and you can make sure it's something worth listening to.

Eliciting the commentary

Set the precedent that the commentary is a vital part of participation in the scheme. If the writing sample is submitted without one, say thanks for the writing and announce that you will consider it as soon as you also have the accompanying commentary. You might pose a question or two (such as those above) to help stimulate this commentary.

Then be sure to respond to this commentary in your own critique. Start by addressing its concerns. Let your mentee know that she is being listened to.

It is good if you can see your development of this written commentary as having equal weight to the development of the mentee's writing samples. Your mentorship is of a limited duration. You want your writer to be fledged and independent at the end of the programme. You want her to have ownership of her writing as well as this process of her own development. As a more experienced writer, your awareness of your own writing process streams as the background to your consciousness every time you sit down to write. This is not so much the case with your mentee. Through these commentaries you have an opportunity to train her into articulate self-awareness of her own writing process. You are bequeathing her a remarkable tool. There is a tendency among less experienced writers to believe that becoming self-conscious about their writing process will somehow destroy the writing itself, that it must well up spontaneously. Experience does not really bear this out for most of us – but even if it is true at some level, it is still useful to learn to distinguish between 'ideas' and 'technique' – no painter, for example, would think that learning how to apply oils to canvas was going to damage their inspiration.

Beyond all that, the mentee's commentary makes mentoring much more alive. You don't have to guess at intentions all the time. You can come to see how the writing has stemmed from a person's struggle. Even if the result seems to be floundering, you can be aware of the heroic battle that lies behind it, the life and the thoughts and the intentions that it emerged through. You will very likely be shaken into new ways of looking at things. You have a lot to give in this mentoring relationship, but also a lot to receive.

Aim to elicit 1,000 words from your mentee. It may well start out as much less than that, but you can help it expand through asking questions for the mentee to answer next time around.

Your critique

How long should it take to write?
You've already prepared in the way outlined in 'Preparing for the Session'. This critique is now your 'session'. If the face-to-face session was to last an hour, you have that to work with. You also have the half-hour each way of travelling time to get to your meeting. That makes two hours for writing your piece. Your mentee is getting two hours of your undivided writing attention. That's quite a sweet deal for the mentee.

How long should it be?
As a rule of thumb, 1,500 to 2,000 words. That includes any of the mentee's words which you import into the narrative of your critique. Make sure you agree a length between the two of you at the start. It's a good idea to include this in your contract.

A step-by-step guide
You'll find some useful ideas just by reading 'The sessions' section. This step-by-step guide is just a model. Follow it at your own convenience and adapt at will.

■ Start the piece like a letter: 'Dear [mentee's first name]'
■ Make some response to the mentee's commentary. Show your interest. Prove that you are listening.
■ Give some qualitative opinion on the submission. Did you like it on the whole? Offer whatever general praise you can.
■ Offer an example of something that pleased you, and say why. Copy the relevant quotation from the mentee's manuscript to your critique.
■ Introduce the major topic you wish to consider in this critique.
■ Offer a positive example, taken from the mentee's work, of how she has already shown signs of achieving the breakthrough you are looking for. As an example: you don't enjoy the likes of 'walked quickly', 'ate greedily', 'looked soulfully'. You want the writer to be alert to her use of

weak verbs plus adverbs. Say why, then search her text and find the word 'gazed'. You have your example of a strong verb, and no adverb.

■ Point out areas where this improvement could be put into effect.

■ Offer a learning anecdote from your own life as a writer. For example, what word did you over-use? What word do you still have a tendency to over-use? It's good to open up in this way. It shows you understand where a writer is coming from. You're stepping down from the podium for a while, allowing yourself to be more personal.

■ Now you relate the material of your anecdote to the mentee's writing. What word might she over-use? Sometimes it can be instructive to use the word search facility to count examples.

■ Say what development most pleased you about the writing. Give details, say why and what effect it has.

■ Point out one other area for development, including a brief example.

■ Summarise your points, highlighting some of the positives.

■ Set a challenge for next time – not so much a writing exercise, just a development you would like to see. Possibly give an example. Use of assonance, for example. Or a place in the text that might have worked better as dialogue.

■ Round off by looking forward to the next submission.

■ Sign off with your first name.

■ Wait a while and re-read your critique before sending it off. You're trying to give a model of good writing, and good proofreading is a part of that. Also check that you have achieved the right tone, one of development plus encouragement. We writers are moody people. Trim your critique of any laments and despair that might have filtered in.

■ Send the piece off as an attachment with just a brief email note. Ask to be informed that the critique has got through safely. Store it in a file.

■ Check your critique arrived safely. Once your mentee has sent note of receipt, rest easy till next time.

Some alternative techniques

Highlights
Use different colours to highlight different elements of work you have imported from the mentee's text.

Track changes
If you are both using Microsoft Word, turn on the 'track changes' facility, to display your edits.

Links

It's always good to suggest related reading matter. Since you're emailing your critique, it's possible to make links directly to places of interest on the internet.

Importing more text

If your mentee has not given you a great deal to work on, it's possible to fulfil your end of the bargain by importing more of her text than you might usually do, making sure to add all the relevant comments. And push for more material from the mentee next time around.

Rewriting

In many ways you are safer knocking words out of a mentee's text than rewriting it. However, sometimes simply rewriting a section is the best way of providing a model of how it might go. Once someone has seen such a model, they can then choose whether to adopt it or not. Make sure to tell them that they are free to use or discard it, that it is an alternative example and not a correction. Think of it as Mozart toying with Salieri's lines. It might be a touch galling, but it's also illuminating – and a lot more useful than Mozart trying to explain himself in words.

Detailed critique

It's best not to go for everything, just to point out certain areas for development. Your mentee might ask you for such a close critique, though, in which case it is fair to import a section of their work and give everything in it your thorough attention, saying what works as well as what does not, and why. Working on a small piece thoroughly in this way is especially helpful when you despair at the amount of work a piece needs. What might seem destructive when applied to the whole, can seem constructive when applied to a segment.

Dr Graham Mort is in charge of postgraduate learning for the creative writing courses at Lancaster University and runs the Distance Learning Creative Writing MA at Lancaster. Lancaster was also the home base for the pan-African distance learning mentoring project, in association with the British Council. Prior to that, Graham pioneered mentoring through distance learning through the Open College of the Arts, and distance learning was also the subject of his PhD.

You pioneered mentoring creative writing through distance learning. What advantages came with that mode of delivery?
The creative writing process is catalytic, it produces big life changes.

Many of the takers for the Open College of the Arts distance learning model were women newly liberated from domestic commitments. Studying was made possible for a whole group whose access to education was restricted, such as women with young children or those who were pregnant. It also opened up new opportunities for those who could not access buildings, such as disabled people, or those with ME, who could not sustain the strain of regular hours. Those in remote geographical locations were also reached – the course was very popular in Orkney, for example. It opened a new constituency of people who could write and become writers. They already had the best ingredient – life experience.

In those days you were working through what we now call 'snail mail'. How did the advent of the word processor change things?
Once something was set in typography, on a page, students were not so keen on revisiting it. The advent of the PC brought the problem that work suddenly looked so good, it looked like it had been published, even though it was incomplete. In virtual form, however, text attains a ductile nature, it becomes malleable. Drawing teachers can lean over a student's shoulder and make a mark on the paper. The process remains kinetic. Working in the virtual realm, the writing mentor can now play a similar role to the visual artist, going back to the electronic version and intervening.

So you see mentors using computers to gain a more hands-on role, directly affecting the mentees' writing?
Intervention by the mentor is easier when attempted virtually. The mentor can use writerly skills to get across ideas about the writing. For example, she might import the mentee's text into her own report and rewrite it. She might rework the layout of a poem or show variant paragraph breaks. She might highlight the number of adjectives to illustrate their over-usage. In prose, she can reset dialogue. Working in the virtual way allows for 'show don't tell'.

Doesn't working through the means of the computer depersonalise the mentor/mentee relationship?
The relationship between the mentor and mentee is dramatised. Their meeting exists in the realm of literature. What is replicated is the very process of reading and writing. The reading/writing polarity is reversed all the time in the cyclical role between the two players. One aspect of working in the virtual realm is that we write our own version of the other person. Both are fictional characters in a narrative. The process of imagining the other student becomes interesting. Email is flirtatious. It also reduces some of the power balance, and is less intimidating for

those in the role of student. It can be disappointing at first when mentors and mentees meet, for each falls short of the other's imagining.

I see the advantage for the mentee in being given the mentor's considered, written report, but isn't it rather time consuming?
Academically, this provision of a mentor's report is an unassailable model, being completely transparent. It does however require an unusual level of commitment by the mentor. It is more intense because it uses *writing* energy. This is both the best and the most draining thing about it.

Distance learning is clearly good for outreach, accessing writers in remote places. How might the internet draw them into a wider sense of literary community?
It's a good idea to back up virtual mentoring with a virtual meeting place. This might allow space for posting profiles, email addresses, discussing reading, and sharing excitements. Through e-learning you can build a resource and create a knowledge base. If you're going to write you must read. Reading has to be embedded in the learning process. Providing an online space for mentees' writings gives them something to write for, but also a bank of relevant and engaged reading materials on which to draw.

Some more questions about being a mentor

In what ways am I in control of the relationship?

In the mentees' section of this book, you will find the onus of maintaining the relationship placed on them. They have the greatest need and the most to lose if the relationship fails. Accordingly, we suggest ways in which they might make allowances for any weaknesses in their mentors so that they can reap full benefit from the mentors' strengths.

However you are the 'senior partner' in an interactive relationship in which two writers are joined for a while. So far as maintaining professional standards means controlling the relationship, then you are in control. Being in control means requiring the work to be done, on both sides, which will strengthen the mentee's writing.

You retain control by extracting the appropriate writing submissions from your mentee and giving them due consideration. You enter each meeting with some clear sense of what you wish to achieve. You come prepared.

The sessions themselves will often try to veer off course. Your mentee is likely to be vulnerable about the writing. This new and more intense focus on writing is likely to rouse emotions in them, which may swirl to the surface and seek to swamp your meeting space. Your main method of control here is to keep returning the focus to the writing. Don't get too distracted into talking about writing in general. Keep coming back to aspects of writing as a craft.

The question of 'who controls the relationship' should hopefully disappear as the sessions continue. As a writer, you should be able to recognise when this has happened. You start off 'in control', then the creative impulse takes over and you can both enjoy the ride.

Even so, it's good to end each session 'in control' with a short plenary. Have the mentee give a quick summary of what has been achieved during the session, prompt as necessary, and make sure the various notes that have been taken are in order.

I like to be encouraging. What happens if I really don't like a piece that's submitted to me?

If this is that first 'trial' piece, to see if you like the writing enough to engage with the mentee, then you don't have to say why you don't like it. Simply say you don't know how you will be able to help. If this dislikeable piece comes later in the process, at least you have a history of liking *something* (that trial piece). You can point out why you preferred one piece of writing to this one.

Remember too, however, that mentoring is not about delivering your opinion. Your role as a mentor is very different from the role of a critic. Nothing is finished yet, so no verdict is called for. You are part of the writer's creative process. Your personal likes and dislikes are real and useful, but they are tools for you to use, not a conclusion.

How rigid do I need to be about keeping to a timetable?

You are your mentee's model of a professional writer, and deadlines are important for writers. Keep to the timetable as much as you can. However you are both adults – unexpected things can happen. You are not bound to institutional regulations, you have some flexibility. If travel takes one of you away for a while, you can consider shifting to distance learning mode for a session or two.

Should I expect my mentee to know my work?

Don't expect it. That opens you to disappointment. You can welcome it, though. It shows initiative and engagement on the mentee's part.

Does it undermine the relationship if I discuss some of my own failures?

No. In Britain especially we tend to warm to people who speak of their failures. However, you are playing a role. Part of that role is being a success. It is easier for the mentee to respect your critique of her work if she can trust your success in the outer world. She wants success herself. Try to stay upbeat and offer stories of success for a while.

It's probably not a good idea to lament the woeful state of publishing, berate your agent, bitch about your advance etc. The idea is to focus on the mentee's writing and help it to develop. Keep the discussion to what helps achieve that goal.

It is good to offer anecdotes from your writing life, from which the mentee might learn useful lessons. These may very well be about things that have gone wrong. Ideally you learned from these 'mistakes' and turned things around. In offering the failure, place it in the context of the whole arc of the experience.

Mentoring means breaking new ground, trying out new skills, and you want your mentee to be unafraid of failure. You might offer tales of times you tried out new skills for the first time.

You do want to encourage rewriting and redrafting. Try relating episodes of when you are at work as an editor on your own writing. What do you cross out, what do you change, and why? Those things that do not survive the editing process are not 'failures', they are part of the writing process. Bring your mentees to understand that.

Is it possible to mentor outside of my own field of writing?

It is possible. You're not then of course mentoring from a position of maximum strength. If you want such a challenge, maybe team up with someone in your own field of writing who is radically different from you.

If you're tired of your own genre, you might look for a mentor in another field and become a mentee.

It's possible that your mentee has not yet discovered her optimum form in which to write. You might discover a poet inside a short story writer, a playwright inside a novelist. That might mean encouraging someone outside the form you know best, and supporting her as she moves on in that new territory.

However, mentoring is also a creative act. If mentoring outside your usual field of writing appeals to you and the mentee, then go for it. If nothing else, you will offer the perspective of a highly informed reader who is a professional with words. If the mentee wishes to break new ground, you will also come with less sense of the restrictions placed by the market for such work.

Graham Mort, while principally writing as a poet, mentors and writes across forms: "Mentoring is one of the few ways you can intervene in a writer's process at an early level, before their writing and mistakes are set in stone. It's one way to save people wasting their lives.

"A poem stands there ready for the mentor, in the same way a motorbike stands there for a mechanic. You can get at it from all sides. Mentoring creates a stimulus for the mentor. You put students down an exciting road and you think, 'Why am I not doing that?' Protagonists can work together – education does not have to be hierarchical. Knowledge is not instilled but mutually explored. The mentor can take her own anxieties as a writer and legitimately explore them through a mentee's work, moving on both their work and her own."

Is it OK to become friends with the mentee?

Of course it's OK. It's bound to happen sometimes. However you do have some duty of care to your mentee. You are in a position of authority. People have different ways of dealing with authority figures, ranging from hostility to adoration. Appreciate that, and don't abuse it. If friendship or intimacy looks on the cards between you and your mentee, it's best to restrict your meetings to the professional ones until the contracted mentoring period is finished. If we're talking intimacy, some people recommend three months between the ending of the formal relationship and the assumption of a more personal one.

How can I guard my own space?

This is an important question for mentors, which is covered elsewhere. Here we would just like to stress the importance of the contract in this regard. Establish and agree the extent and the limitation of your relationship at the beginning and you have something to refer back to later, should things go awry. Part of your role as a mentor is giving an example of how a writer's time is valuable and needs protection.

Do I have to mark work?

Elsewhere we discuss how to write comments on a manuscript. Do you give the work a grade? No. As mentors we're not about passing judgment. We're about making work stronger.

How do I measure success?

Comparing a piece of writing from the end of the mentoring period to one from the beginning should give you some measure of that success.

What does the mentee feel she's gained? If nothing, then maybe you have a failure on your hands. If she feels she's improved, that's success. The degree to which she can articulate exactly how she has improved is a real success. A vital goal of mentoring, one that sometimes gets overlooked, is the way the mentee becomes more conscious of her writing craft and how she is applying it.

You might take a passage from early in the mentoring process and one from the end and see if the mentee can see and explain how one is stronger than the other – and be ready with your own explanation just in case she cannot see it!

Did you *both* enjoy the mentorship? Did you take pleasure in the writing, and feel gratified when points you made were absorbed? Then that is a success.

Should I feel responsible for helping my mentee become published?

It may have been one of your mentee's agreed goals to become 'more publishable', in which case you might take market considerations into account when reviewing the work. Elsewhere we consider why it can be helpful to separate issues of publication from the mentoring process.

You have a professional history of interchange with the publishing industry. It's good to pass on some of that wisdom. You may well be the only published writer your mentee knows. Any experience you have to offer can be useful.

You might want to make publication possibilities an issue in your final session, as you consider where the mentee goes next with her writing.

Writers' relationships with their agents and editors are increasingly vulnerable. It seems best to us to use the mentoring contract to specifically exclude such introductions. Make exceptions if you want to, but we would expect these to be rare exceptions.

How many drafts of the same piece should I see before moving on to something new?

One. The original one. The idea is that the mentee uses input from one piece of writing to inform the next piece. It's best not to get stuck on perfecting one section. It's also hard to come fresh to a piece you have already read several times and commented upon at length.

What happens if I keep having to make the same points again and again?

Accept the fact that the point is not getting through and move on to something else. You're not instructing when you are a mentor. You are offering feedback and guidance. No one is obliged to take it.

Should I recommend reading other writers?

Consider whether your mentee will have easy access to the recommended books first, but yes, it's a good idea. We all learn from reading others, so it's valuable to be given specific advice as to which authors we might learn from.

If you feel a point you want to make is best illustrated by another writer, you might take a photocopy of a particular page into the session with you for your mentee to take away. Make sure she understands what she might gain from the writing, and how to apply it to her own work.

How much hand-holding do I have to do?

Writing is a tough business. Your mentee may well already have ample experience of that fact. As a mentor you are working on the writing, not on the business.

You are likely to meet as strangers, and both of you may well be nervous at that first meeting. The mentee is likely to be the more nervous of the two, with their writing on the line. It is good to be a little protective and encouraging at first, as your relationship establishes itself. This gives the mentee the room to learn to trust you, to know you won't savage her work, and therefore the scope to be more adventurous. She doesn't need to impress you each time. And you don't have to like what you are shown. Once you have established solid ground, criticism can be accepted as kindly rather than hostile.

What happens if a piece seems really good and I can't see ways of improving it?

Enjoy the challenge! The best writing is often the hardest work for the mentor, but can be really rewarding. Read once for pleasure and simply savour the experience. Then read it again critically. You loved the whole, but what elements are not quite up to the excellence of others, and why? You will find something useful to say.

However, do not be shy of simply saying where and why something works so well. How often have you had such sustained and careful praise of your own writing? How wonderful would it be? It's liberating to be shown our own strengths. It allows us to really stretch our talent.

What's the best way of knowing what the mentee is trying to achieve?

Ask her.

Should I set assignments?

Some mentors do set writing exercises. That involves being a personal tutor as well as a mentor. It is usually enough for the mentee to go away from the feedback in one session, knowing what new skills she might apply in the writing she will submit for the next.

Mentoring for Performance

Gerry Potter mentors writers towards performance. His approach to mentoring is intuitive, based on experience and passionate encouragement, and draws writers into giving voice to the words that lie silent on the paper so they can learn to recognise what is 'true'. This section aims to help mentors who focus on performance. Gerry cheerfully subverts some of the 'rules' for mentoring established in this book, to real success, so everyone might gain something from reading about his approach.

Gerry Potter is an actor, poet, performer and playwright. He also writes and performs as Chloe Poems – or maybe she writes and performs through him. Chloe is working on a book of deranged autobiography in which she and Gerry mix voices and genres. Gerry's latest Arts Council England mentoring project sees him guiding six poets towards joint book publication and DVD performance.

Gerry's 'mentees' – distrusting that word, Gerry prefers 'colleagues' – know of his work and seek him out. When he started this work five years ago, the very word 'mentor' was frightening, much too 'big' with a guru-like feel to it. "People want a bit of your body of work, and suddenly you realise you know things. It's very encouraging. I liked developing a relationship with that 'mentor' word, which seems bigger than what you do. Taking on board the word brings a certain responsibility – the very act of mentoring mentors you. You've got to be good, and honest, and aware in so many dimensions."

Mentoring has an outreach side to it, connecting with writers who are marginalised by the regular educational channels. Gerry made his own alternative way to success, which helps him be especially accessible to such writers. "I don't come from a taught background. I left school at 15, can't even spell properly, don't know how to write poetry in a proper sense – but I write poetry. People who choose me want to be freer in how they write and perform. They are restricted by how they have been taught, all so structured and so tight.

"My approach is very improvised – I don't know anything in that formal way, I only know what I know. I look at work beforehand but I improvise, nothing is terribly prepared. This stems from my training at the Everyman Youth Theatre in Liverpool, improvising constantly. It honed that listening instinctive skill that I have. I never come to a session with reams of paper. I want it to be *theirs*. Some have said to me, 'People have given me tomes to read and you don't. It makes it so much easier.' It's a kind of relief for them. I sometimes think that books bully. I'd never say, 'Go and read *1984*,' so they're faced with this magnificent book. I've found that can make people not write, scared to do so, because someone else has done it first or done it better.

"When I listen to writers read aloud or perform their own writing, I know instinctively what's working. A lot of language has a truth, and I recognise what is true. Then they'll change the material around it so as to fit in with what works. It's not about saying what's right or wrong, just saying what's true. Even with playwrights I ask them to read their work aloud so I can hear it and get an instinctive understanding of it. Because we talk, language has to be heard. Books are silent voices. It's about putting the voice into words, finding where that voice comes from, what it does. Language becomes more real when it's spoken.

"When I encourage writers to read to me it gives them confidence. Writers can be too silent and self-absorbed. There's a place for that, but you then have to create the sounds. When it's spoken you'll know intuitively if something works.

"I like untaught, instinctive writing. I like those I'm mentoring to see that *they* have a relationship with the work, they created it, they are mini-Gods. People don't say that to them, and I find that really sad.

"People are not told how important it is to have an idea. Also they are not told that writing is emotional. People like to achieve and be encouraged. Writing is isolating and lonely. I instigate conversations about writing and what writing means, ask, 'Why do you want this voice?' and have emotional conversations about the practice. I'm also happy, though, for people to get angry and frustrated by the mentoring process. That's an emotional response; it's a relationship, it's positive for there to be fury or frustration.

"I do a *lot* of talking. I generally like people's work and have a real relationship to it; I'm very enthused, and able to go on some energetic level with it. I tend to bring an emotive edge to my mentoring, and have to hold it back a bit.

"Occasionally I have to say to someone, 'What you love isn't working,' though I coat the criticism in positivity. I say it when language is either stagnant or clumsy. When someone doesn't know *why* they've written something, it's a lazy moment.

"Success is when a piece becomes fuller. It has its place and says what it has to say, and does not oversay it. People get that when you've shown them.

"Playwriting is easiest to mentor – I write plays that have done very well on The Fringe. I have an actor's temperament first and foremost.

I like to see characters come alive and develop the undercurrents of plot. I'm happy to write with the writers as well. I'm mentoring Dominic Berry with his play about lonely gays in pubs, who drink too much, which grew out of some performance poems I also helped him with. He has allowed me, generously, to extend his ideas and offer a lot of input. If I've extended it, the idea has still come from him, it's still his work and not mine. Most people I've worked with have let me do that. It makes me happy; it's a very sharing working process, nothing didactic.

"Poets come to me, and I'm more cautious with poetry. I don't want to rubbish the world of poetry, though free-form poetry is my own line. I do say there's been enough poetry about leaves, sky and grass. Give me real personal poetry from experience, political poetry, poetry with bite. I can't bear yet another 'horrific coming out to my family' poem and that kind of thing. I tell them, 'This has been done and can't be done again.' As soon as you say that they move away from it.

"You can put performance poetry on the page; you just have to be careful about how. Rather than just be confessional or conversational, you can focus on the language and seek to make it more poetic.

"Mentoring helps my own work. Sometimes you hear yourself say things that you take on board. When you hear someone say something that really works you think, 'I want a bit of that.' You don't steal, but you may borrow. Also if someone's asked for you as a mentor it means you really have to pull your intellectual socks up. *You've* got to be confident – that's the most important thing. It can be scary assuming that confidence when you first start out.

"Mentoring *is* a relationship. It's a threesome – the writer, the work, and me. You develop a familial bond. I like mentoring in people's homes – with tea and biscuits. More often than not I'll stay longer than an hour and have fun. I stay longer because I like it, and it makes me more human and approachable. I'm happy to chat about their lives and relationships. What's not said and what's not on the page is as vivid and entertaining as what's on the page. We laugh about the work, not at it. Laughter and a sense of fun are important, even with the most urgent and dense work."

For managers

You understand the benefits of mentoring, but where do you start when setting up a scheme? In this section, you can find out how to establish, manage and evaluate a successful mentoring scheme, enabling you and your organisation to support the development of emerging and established writers in your region.

Support for writers

"Mentoring is an important aspect of professional development; with a basis in dialogue, it allows flexibility for both mentor and mentee to work out their own programme and processes, for mutual learning. With careful brokerage and support, the mentoring experience can facilitate quite divergent ways to address very different creative and professional challenges and needs."
Jonathan Meth, director of writernet

One of the things that surprised and delighted us as we began to research this book was the remarkable range of both 'providers' (managers) and of provision in this field. It is hard to suggest outlines of good practice that are going to apply to everyone – from, say, mentoring for a single playwright within the context of a theatre residency to an online scheme like Crossing Borders, which mentored over 300 emerging writers with no face-to-face contact whatsoever. Different organisations go into mentoring with different agendas and therefore different practices. It is quite difficult at first glance to see what a scheme like the Jerwood/Arvon experiment, with a pre-set number of highly qualified mentees (MA students in this case) experiencing mentoring within a firm and time-limited structure, share with an on-going individual process like New Writing North's or with a mentoring scheme run to enhance or enrich the lives of a specific group. However, we hope that a wider understanding of how other people are using this particular form of professional development will be helpful.

Why might I want to get involved in mentoring?
Mentoring in fields other than creative writing has proved effective in supporting professional and personal development, retaining staff, learning new skills, and developing self-esteem. The USA business experience suggests that it is particularly effective in redressing imbalances within the traditional workforce (ethnic minorities and women have been the usual categories examined, because of the anti-discrimination legislation). These benefits appear to work across the board – mentors and the overall 'office environment' seem to gain in these areas as well as the individual mentees. Of course it is more or less impossible to measure 'success' in these terms within creative writing, but it is reasonable to suppose – and this is anecdotally supported – that the effects flow from this particular approach to

professional development rather than from the specific environment. This in itself seems a sound basic reason for literature developers to learn more about mentoring. However there are other reasons to get involved.

Presently there seems to be a gap in provision for emerging writers. Despite the fact that we writers are constantly complaining about it, there has been reasonable funding through bursaries and through community projects, but both of these do have limitations. Most bursary funding is necessarily pinned to one-off projects, which are already in a fairly advanced stage of development. The usual requirement for novelists for instance is 10,000 words in a shape worthy of submission. This does suit some writers but not all. It is hard on newer writers who may find being on their own with the money they thought they wanted is destabilising and imposes a particular sort of pressure, which is not necessarily helpful. It also, perhaps more importantly, militates against serious experiment and a proper developmental phase.

Community projects and residencies are also invaluable, but if seriously undertaken do tend to be both engaging and labour intensive. Too often they do not in fact create real creative time for many writers. In 1999, as a preparation for The Year of the Artist, the then East Midlands Arts took very seriously their commitment to creating a 'practitioners advisory group' (across the art forms) and it was interesting that the sort of residencies that artists favoured differed slightly from the expectations of development officers – in particular, most artists generally favoured short and intense projects over long-term residencies as being more supportive of their own practice.

Meanwhile, of course, there are many excellent workshops and learning opportunities at every level – and these too are important, indeed crucial, provision, but obviously they cannot offer an emerging writer ongoing individual attention or a place to look at their work in a wider context.

At its simplest, mentoring can offer a new tier of development to individual writers at a great many points in their careers. At the moment, mentoring is gaining considerable interest both within the arts community and more widely. Developing mentoring schemes and projects is therefore a high profile approach; there are various funding channels (as we will discuss later in this chapter) available at the moment; the people who have set up such schemes are expressing a high level of satisfaction; and writers are increasingly looking for structures in which they can obtain this kind of training.

Supporting new writers

The feedback from writers who have received mentoring seems to be extremely favourable. On the whole this evidence is anecdotal as there has been very little overall evaluation done, and probably the process is still too new for this to be useful. However, many post-mentoring writers have responded to our request for comments and some of these seem particularly relevant here:

"I think [mentoring has] helped me to face some of my blind spots. I used to take a very aesthetic approach to writing, in the sense that I focused on striking images, unusual metaphors and other special effects. [My mentor] helped me to see that these were sometimes rococo and overdone. He also guided me to focus on other crucial aspects of the novel that I'd been neglecting, including three-dimensional characters, thoroughly imagined surroundings and a coherent and plausible plot. He touched on these themes often, gently bringing me back as I kept veering off towards my old habits.

"So when I write now, I have a wider set of concerns in mind than simply an arresting phrase or picture. I hope that will make my finished manuscript a much better work than it would otherwise have been.

"I received a great deal of insightful feedback, plenty to keep me going as I continued my writing. The end did not feel like an abandonment. I have been writing at a good pace since then."
Greg Fried, Crossing Borders participant

"The programme certainly strengthened my sense of identity as a writer. With my mentor taking my writing so seriously, responding to it critically, I began to do so as well."
John Lazarus, Crossing Borders participant

There is another group of writers for whom mentoring offers a real opportunity: writers established in one form who would like to develop their work in radically new directions: poets who wish to explore narrative fiction; novelists who want to write for the stage or for radio; established short story writers who are being pressured towards a novel; writers who are experiencing some sort of 'block' or feel stuck in a rut. It can be difficult for more established writers to attend evening classes or join groups – there is always a tendency towards rivalry and their success may be resented by other members of a group. Working with a writer at a similar career point but in a different form can prove invaluable and inspirational. They are also deeply satisfying to work *with* from a mentor's point of view.

The biographer Carole Angier points out the need for mentoring for writers of non-fiction:

"Non-fiction mentoring is undervalued. Non-fiction writers need more help than anyone else. There is such a technical element to non-fiction; for example, how do you research through the web, through the British Library, through the National Archives at Kew? A mentoring period with a biographer might mean writing only one complete chapter, for it is largely a guide on how to do research."

Writers are seeking mentoring, they are enjoying mentoring and they appear to be getting a lot of professional value from mentoring at various different stages of their careers. This is probably a major reason for literature development managers to get involved in mentoring.

Supporting more established writers
Mentoring schemes offer a 'two for the price of one' deal for the hard-pressed literature development officer!

As well as supporting and developing the emergent writer, mentoring also offers a range of real benefits to the mentors. For those writers who enjoy the process, mentoring is a strongly positive experience. First, of course, it is paid work – paid work that values the writer for *being a writer* (rather than for some other quality – such as teaching or running workshops) is extremely affirmative.

"As a mentor [each] session *is* about sharing all I know in the world – writing. The only person to really value that is someone who only writes. To share all of that, to see someone grappling with all of that, is morale boosting.

"Mentees do tend to read my work. It's the only time I feel really well read – critics don't do it. I'll be working with mentees and they bring up examples from my own work to illustrate a point I have just made, and that feels wonderful."
Jill Dawson

Moreover, mentoring is work that comes with built-in flexibility and leaves writers with a good deal of control over their own time and space in a way that, for example, a weekly evening workshop does not. Even the extremely reclusive or isolated writer can access mentoring online or through a few controlled forays into one-to-one situations.

The financial and professional aspects of mentoring are very important, but there are other significant benefits. It is enriching and affirming to be a mentor in ways that teaching a class does not come near. Mentoring gives a writer time and space to reflect on their own process, to become aware of their own depth of experience and to talk about the business of writing.

"I am deeply grateful to my mentees. I know that working with them has strengthened my own writing in various ways. Some of these are specific – I learned a great deal about narrative and how even very 'literary' fiction can relate to its oral roots and rhythms from working on Crossing Borders; I see that coming through in my own short stories. But the greatest gain for me has been something more general. Mentoring has enabled me to reflect on my own process at a very precise point. I have been able to become more self-conscious about the whole activity without having to make my own work self-conscious. In mentoring you don't have to be right or wrong – you never have to assess or mark other writers' work, only talk and think about writing itself. There is a shared learning curve. This new self-awareness gives me confidence and makes me freer."
Sara Maitland

The idea that established writers like mentoring and want to deepen their skills in this area is reflected in Jill Dawson's experience with The Writers' Pool, a mentoring project she co-ran for the Royal Literary Fund, from 2003 to 2004. In one sense this was an unusual scheme because it began with the mentors, rather than the mentees (see below). The large number of established writers, including those with substantial 'seniority', who wished to be involved in the project showed how creating such a mentoring scheme can offer specific and welcome provision for established writers, and especially those who may be having a difficult time with their own work.

"Many mentors maybe had their heyday when younger; they are now going through a rough patch, and have a great deal of experience to bring. We *ought* to value those people – their experience, their productivity, their continued creative productiveness. All writers' lives are in cycles. Being valued as a mentor can help writers through fallow periods, and perhaps trigger the next stage in their careers."
Jill Dawson

Encouraging diversity
Currently, and in our opinion rightly, there is a real commitment, reflected in many arts policy statements and funding strands, to providing access

to the arts for groups who have been traditionally under-represented. As we suggested in the introductory chapter, in the USA, mentoring in the business world evolved partly in response to the requirement imposed by the various anti-discrimination laws to address under-representation. The effectiveness of this one-to-one approach to personal development has a track record of success in other fields and it is reasonable to suppose this will work for writers as well.

Glaydah Namukasa, the Ugandan writer who won the 2005 Macmillan Prize for children's writing with her novel *Voice of a Dream*, has been very open about the importance of mentoring to her and her peers – and incidentally shows the importance of being clear about your own goals: "I said I wanted to write for young adults and I wanted my writing to get to an international level. I also said that I was aiming to win writing competitions and one of them was the Macmillan... My sincere thanks go to my mentor, who started with me right from the beginning when I didn't even know the difference between structure and plot."

Mentoring offers a very precise way of accessing voices from groups that may have been silenced, both as one-off writer-to-writer arrangements and as regional or national projects.

Spread the Word, a London-based literature development organisation, for example, is in the process of developing a large-scale national mentoring scheme which will start in 2007 to address the needs of Black and Asian poets. In 2005, Arts Council England commissioned them to conduct research into the under-representation of this group in poetry publishing as compared to other art forms. (The findings from this research were published as *Free Verse*, 2006.) To many of the 226 poets surveyed, the difficulties appeared structural, or "a resistant publishing context, a lack of role models, a sense of demoralisation and low self-confidence, and a real need for support and development".

In response to this, Spread the Word has been working towards a two-year development programme, called *The Complete Works*, which will consist of mentoring, plus a mini-conference series. The goal is for 15 poets each to produce a publishable collection of poetry. As Spread the Word's information sheet puts it:

"Each poet will have a mentor drawn from an internationally known pool of published poets with a track record in mentoring, such as Kwame Dawes, Simon Armitage, Eavan Boland, Mimi Khalvati and Steven Knight. Each mentee will meet face-to-face with their mentor at least three times each year and will also have email and phone contact where necessary and appropriate. Contracts will be drawn up between mentors and mentees to ensure both parties are clear about the expectations and boundaries of the relationship."

This is a substantial commitment in terms of time and resources, and suggests a confidence in the benefits of mentoring for particular excluded groups.

Group mentoring schemes

Here we are going to look at a selection of formal mentoring arrangements, which seem to us to have been successful. Our intention is to show the range and the diversity of provision and to encourage individuals or organisations to develop these ideas further, or to come up with new structures to meet their own particular agenda.

The Writers' Pool (2003-2004)

The Writers' Pool was a project funded by The Royal Literary Fund, and managed by Jill Dawson as a Royal Literary Fund Fellow. This was a fairly tightly managed scheme, with 10 meetings organised between the mentors and mentees and with a strong focus on supporting mentors as much as mentees. The mentors were all Royal Literary Fund Fellows and the scheme tended to use senior mentors with a real body of work behind them. Mentees were chosen on the basis of their submitted work and a brief covering letter.

"Mentors were sent a selection of pieces by prospective mentees from which to make their choice. Later, the Writers' Pool moved on to having the mentors select their own mentees.

 "Writers' Pool ran events in which the 10 mentors and mentees all met together, and one in which they met to celebrate the end. They were pretty much all-day events, with food and wine. At the first, all the various permutations of the course were discussed, the procedures to follow and the problems that might arise. This happened after the mentor and mentee had met for the first of their ten private meetings, in which the mentor discussed the initial piece on the basis of which they had chosen the mentee. The final event was held in a central venue, with an invited audience including agents and editors, in which mentors introduced their mentees who then read from their work."

Jill Dawson

In outline, this is a common model. Jan Rutherford runs a broadly similar scheme for Scottish writers through Words@Work at the **Scottish Book Trust** – advertising publicly for participants in both roles; matching mentors and mentees in what look like appropriate pairings, which are inevitably governed in part by geography; organising an induction day and binding the participants to a fairly rigorously defined number of meetings and providing a timetable for them.

The **Jerwood/Arvon** joint mentoring scheme is similarly structured. However the mentees here are already studying creative writing at a post-graduate level and are selected by their university tutors as exceptionally talented. Instead of an initial induction day these mentoring relationships start with a full week's masterclass at one of the Arvon Centres. Again the structure is tightly organised and the relationships last for six months with approximately monthly meetings. (See *Young Writers' Apprenticeships 2004/05* (Worple Press) for a full report of this project.)

This is currently the most usual model for a mentoring project offered by a literature organisation. The managers take a strong leadership role in the project, firstly in recruiting both mentors and mentees, and then in shepherding both sides through a fairly streamlined, timetabled programme. In these schemes the mentees are selected broadly on merit, as demonstrated in work they have already produced.

New Writing North

Claire Malcolm, the director of New Writing North, uses mentoring in a completely different way. She has been using mentoring for writers' development since 1998, but does not run a project or scheme of the previous kind. New Writing North sets up mentoring partnerships to support individual writers whom she feels may profit from this approach: that is to say she selects mentoring for specific writers, rather than mentees for mentoring schemes. Within that framework she allows the partners to work out their own methods – frequency, timing and indeed overall number of meetings, length of submission, type of input, and overall direction are left to be negotiated freely by the two writers involved. At any given time she may have up to seven mentoring partnerships at work, but there is no co-ordination between them, nor any particular type of writer she is 'targeting'. This is a writer-centred approach, and one which allows her to develop mentoring across the whole range of genres and forms. Each partnership has a closing date and both sides must create reports of the work done. The mentors are paid and have a contract with New Writing North, but in most other respects this approach probably comes as near as professional relationships can to the traditional friendship mentoring that has always existed between writers: Malcolm is functioning perhaps like the hostess of a salon!

Sara Maitland has mentored several times for New Writing North:

"Writing about Claire's approach makes me feel a bit uncomfortable because it is hard to pin down exactly what she *does do*. 'Makes introductions and pays bills' makes it sound so easy. Her support and availability is constant – and if I were to fail to deliver I expect I would have her on my doorstep pretty quickly – but when things are moving forward she seems pretty much invisible. New Writing North pays its mentors in three separate phases over the agreed mentoring period, and to get paid you have to submit a report, so there is a strong impetus towards reasonable record keeping and a way for Claire to keep an eye on the whole process. For me, though, it is the perfect way to work – I feel that both I and my mentees get a good chance to 'choose' each other although in almost every case they are not people I would have met socially or without New Writing North's involvement. Having a strong management behind (or around) me allows me to develop the personal and affirmative aspects that are central to both the effectiveness and the fun of mentoring without any fear that I will end up at the mercy of some needy or greedy writer (including, of course, myself!). I suspect that for this approach to work you need a manager who knows the pool of writers-as-potential-mentors well because success depends on good matching of the parties. It also depends on having years of networking experience in the region and of monitoring similar schemes. This may mean that it is a regional approach – and indeed requires a region where the writers' infrastructure is strong. When it does work, however, it seems to me ideal."
Sara Maitland

It seems likely that this model will develop further because of the Arts Council England grant input, which means individual writers will be seeking mentors directly, rather than places on a mentoring scheme and because it will probably prove the easiest model for commercial mentoring as that takes off. For example, *Chapter and Verse*, The Literary Consultancy's mentoring scheme launched in 2007 with support from Arts Council England, essentially uses this model, although delivery is by email rather than direct contact, and the commercial clients are self-selecting.

Mentoring and diversity
As we have already suggested, one particular use of mentoring has been to develop work within communities which have traditionally been excluded from arts practice.

For example, Graeae, the theatre company of actors with physical or sensory disabilities, ran a mentoring scheme for dramatists in 1999-2000 and followed this up with a project called DisPlay 4 (2001-02), which it describes as apprenticeships, but which built on the mentoring project.

Writernet, a comprehensive support and development organisation for dramatic writers, was a partner with Graeae in these projects and has also supported other mentoring opportunities for playwrights from specific communities.

There have, over the last 10 years, been mentoring schemes for a very large range of such groups. They are usually set up and managed by organisations that already have an engagement or involvement with an 'excluded' community, as much as by literature development agencies. The problem for writers has been that such projects tend to be one-offs and not always easy to find out about. Almost inevitably they have explicit deadlines for submission and attendance – it is all too easy for writers in the target communities to miss the information, or to be unable to use the opportunity at the moment it is available. However, Arts Council England (and its Scottish, Welsh and Northern Irish equivalents) have been supportive of this kind of mentoring, and it seems an area in which partnerships between the communities' own organisations and literature agencies could usefully be developed further.

One problem with promoting writing from under-represented groups is locating potential talent: the nature of exclusion means that some minority groups may not access the arts through the usual channels. Clearly one task of literature development is to connect with these groups and facilitate their access to mainstream arts and enable their specific new voices to be heard. Mentoring is a very effective way of doing this.

"One way of having outreach to the new voices from new communities is to use the writers you choose as mentors as conduits. Writers are part of different communities, and will be approached by people within those communities. Selecting mentors from outside the mainstream, and then having them select their own mentees, is one effective way of reaching new voices. A way of establishing fairness is that sample writings from those mentees are still submitted for judgment, so as to be sure that those potential mentees have something that can be developed, even if the primary initial evidence is energy."
Jill Dawson

In Zimbabwe, Ignatius Mabasa, one of the country's leading young writers in Shona, managed a successful mentoring scheme for three years (2003-2006) funded by The British Council. Matching writers from across the country with others overseas, Mabasa's experience offers a very useful model for others seeking to set up and run a nationwide mentoring project.

How did you first promote the scheme to writers?
Writers were sought through adverts in national papers. Writers' organisations were also approached, but alerted that they could be shown no special favours.

Did you set any limits on those who could apply?
The initial programme was for the under-35s, but this went against our policy of open access. In fact, the more mature writers were more committed and focused.

How did you process writers' applications?
Applicants submitted three works by email. There were 900-plus applicants for 12 places each year. They were assessed by independent judges, who were asked to write a few lines of comment on each applicant. A generic response was sent to those who did not succeed, pointing out high levels of competition. They were entered on a database and kept posted on developments in the literary world.

How easy was it for writers to adapt to being mentored?
Mentees were very worried about their first assignment. It felt like starting a journey without knowing your destination. Mentors did manage to criticise in a way that still gave hope. Even so, after that first assignment many mentees said, "I won't write again." *Then* they took on board the comments they had been given, rather than resisting them. From that point on they recognised they were entering on a journey of self-discovery. Mentoring built on skills that they already possessed. The process was more like one of negotiation with the mentor, discussing and improving on what the writer believed was good writing.

Outside the obvious fact that it enabled writers to meet over vast geographical distances, what were the other benefits of distance learning?
Distance learning by email works. It means the work is not under pressure, it leaves time to digest, and it is cost-effective too.

How effective was mentoring?

A new generation of writers, born in the city and so not having that transition from country to city to deal with, is not being heard. There is a hunger to hear them, but there is a drought in publishing. Publishers bring out one or two novels a year. Manuscripts are returned unread. Mentoring gave these writers the confidence to say, yes, I am a writer. I can write.

Publishers learned about the programme and asked about promising writers. Writers have been published as a result of the mentoring, and won residencies abroad.

What did you do to maintain the benefits of the programme once it ended?

A database is maintained, so that the emerging writers are kept informed of any new courses, events or developments in literature. The organisation values them dropping by and letting us know what they are achieving in terms of publication. Also we are creating a 'memory wall', to capture what people feel the scheme did for them.

We mean to develop a website, where people can post stories and keep in contact with each other. We also hope to gain funds to publish work from writers on the programme.

Workshops brought participants together. Mentoring helped to form new groups of writers, and some of these have got together to adopt schools in their local areas, setting up or working with writing clubs.

National Association for Writers in Education, National Association for Literature Development and Lapidus

Anne Caldwell has run a series of mentoring programmes for writers for these development organisations. They are radically different from most other mentoring schemes because they are specifically about career and skills development, rather than about writing in the text-based sense.

The take-up for these programmes has been enthusiastic; this sort of training is obviously valuable. Interestingly it more closely mirrors the original corporate business understanding of mentoring than the creative text-based approaches, which are what most people think of when they think about mentoring as part of literature development.

In short, a very large number of organisations, both those directly involved with literature development and those who represent particular interest groups have used mentoring schemes to a large number of ends. There are very few rules here, but there is a method widely supported by writers which is demonstrably effective.

Do I need to set up a specific scheme?

You don't *need* to do anything! However if you decide to get involved in supporting writers through mentoring, you probably do want to think through various possible strategies. Of course these approaches are not mutually exclusive.

If you want to direct your attention to individual writers who are already *en route,* including mid-career or even very well-established writers who want some extra support (these can often be writers who are interested in working in a new form or developing some particular new area of skill) then there are obvious advantages in taking the New Writing North approach and not setting up a one-off tightly run scheme. Even working this way, however, you will probably want to think into the future a bit. Experience brings confidence and knowledge.

Claire Malcolm's experience at New Writing North would seem to support this. She created her first mentoring partnership in 1997/98 for poet Subhadassi (the mentee) and Andy Croft (the mentor). Subhadassi had come to her wanting to become more independent of 'the day job' and become a full-time writer, and mentoring was something Malcolm thought she could offer him. Initially she saw it as a 'professional friendship', but the benefits the two writers appeared to gain from the relationship started her thinking about how to use mentoring elsewhere. With nearly 10 years of experience, she knows a pool of writers who feel that mentoring is useful to them as well as the mentee and who have demonstrated an ability to deliver. She has developed a clear framework for contracts and support for both parties – including ways of accessing feedback and assessment; she has a knowledge of funding sources and above all, as she puts it, a "community network", which addresses the clear need of writers who otherwise can find themselves in the wilderness. Claire's well-grounded belief that mentoring works for everyone involved is the fruit of experience. Although she has no "specific scheme" she has "a highly flexible tool for literature development" which is open to further exploration.

Equally there are strong cases for setting up particular projects. These might include a strategic decision to open doors for particular communities where you are not in touch with the writers within those communities – you cannot easily set up one-to-one relations unless the writers are approaching you. With a well-focused scheme, for example, you can attract applications from beyond your own database through targeted advertising. Or you might locate a specific funding source, or wish to raise your profile locally or nationally. If your remit is wider than a regional one, or you are not aware of how much enthusiasm there might be for mentoring on either side within your writing community, a tightly organised scheme may well answer those questions. Another advantage of a specific project is that it can put a group of emerging writers in touch *with each other*. Jan Rutherford, who manages a mentoring scheme for Scottish writers, feels this is one of the most important parts of the scheme – many writers in rural areas can feel totally isolated; through mentoring they not only gain professional support but they also gain a community.

Most of the organisations that have run mentoring schemes stress the importance of the 'induction day' and/or a celebration day at the end; some schemes offer a website or chat room for members. A structured project means that there will be a group of writers at a similar point in their careers sharing a particular form of development. Making this point of connection conscious for the writers is itself an important part of building up writers' communities and nourishing supportive networks. Obviously these benefits can be most easily and explicitly drawn upon where there is a well-focused mentoring scheme involving a reasonably sized group of participants.

What do I actually do?

In the first instance, you may have to design and justify the scheme, and then raise and manage the necessary funds.

Once the project exists on paper, you will need to:

■ Recruit appropriate mentors and mentees
■ Ensure that both sides understand what is involved and have the tools to carry out their part
■ Match mentees and mentors with each other and bring them together
■ Organise payment for the mentors – this probably means issuing contracts
■ Monitor progress and arrange for some form of feedback/final assessment
■ Be prepared to mediate or support if there are difficulties in the relationship
■ Support and celebrate the end of the formal partnership

How do I identify suitable mentors?

There are two different ways to tackle this. If you have already identified writers you want to provide with mentors, you will be looking for someone whom you think this particular writer, at this particular point in their career, with these particular aims, will get the most out of. In this situation it is worth asking the potential mentee if she has any ideas, but beyond that you are fairly dependent on the writers you know or are in contact with.

The other way to find mentors is perhaps more common: here you have a mentoring scheme with a particular focus – but you probably do not yet have any individual mentees.

There are various approaches to identifying suitable individuals. Public advertising, through local networks or nationally as appropriate, seems a particular good way of approaching this, as it may put you in contact with excellent writers whom you did not know, or whom you had not imagined might be interested. It also seems 'just'. If you have specific writers you would like to work with it is always worth bringing the advertisement to their direct attention. Any advertisement should outline the scheme and clarify the anticipated level of engagement you are looking for. Criteria worth thinking about might include:

■ Applicants should be published (or in other forms – playwriting, for example – demonstrate some other form of professional competence and achievement).
■ Applicants should have some experience of teaching creative writing.
■ Applicants should provide references.
■ Any project-specific requirements – for example, if delivery is to be by email, some level of IT competence might be necessary.

You need to be prepared for a very strong response. Every manager we have spoken to who used national advertising has found a remarkably high level of applications.

Obviously, the shortlisted candidates need to be interviewed – though if you are looking for a large group of mentors, particularly if you are searching nationally, these interviews could be by telephone. As yet, there is no clear pattern as to who will make a good mentor, but there are some characteristics that a manager might want to consider:

■ Mentors seem to work best when they believe that they will get something useful out of it for themselves as writers. Does an applicant convince you that they feel they had something to gain as well as something to give? In schemes where the mentees already exist, the mentors need to be excited by the individual mentee's writing. In generic schemes, the 'gain' will inevitably be nebulous.
■ Good mentors need to have a critical tolerance, coupled with curiosity. They are not being asked to turn a mentee into a specific kind of writer, but to enable a mentee to be their own 'best writer'.
■ Mentors need to be secure without being arrogant about their own work. It is essential to effective mentoring that mentors do not need to

project themselves too much onto their mentees. This is not necessarily about 'success' – many writers mentor during difficult periods in their own careers, but they still need a basic confidence about their own worth as writers. This may be one reason why publication is a necessary criterion for mentoring.

■ Generosity of spirit. A mentor needs to have the generosity of imagination to see and respect what a writer is trying to achieve: perhaps a simple ability to rejoice in someone's else's excellence and success without wanting to own it.

■ Technical skill and ability to work alone, one-to-one, over a sustained period.

The most common cause for a breakdown in mentoring is a mismatch between the mentor and the mentee. This means that to manage a mentoring scheme effectively you have to have at least a good sense of the overall style and personality of both parties.

"Maybe it would have been better if the manager had a brief personal meeting with them as well, for since breakdowns happen on issues of personality clashes, the personality is more likely to be intuited from a meeting. One possibility is a day course providing something for all applicants and mentors, before the selection process happens, so everyone gets something but there is a chance to scope out the individual personalities beforehand. The ongoing mentoring would come out of the initial course."
Jill Dawson

Obviously as a manager you will build up your own profile of a good mentor, but these comments may give you something to start with.

How do I identify appropriate emerging writers?
The usual method is to advertise as widely as is appropriate to your plan, and invite would-be mentees to submit a sample of their writing and some description of where they feel they are as writers, why they are interested in having a mentor and what they hope to get out of it. This is the easy bit! All managers who have used this approach have had plenty of choice when it comes to selecting their participants. If you are trying to engage with a specific community and are not getting a reasonable volume of applications, the probability is that your advertising strategy is at fault, or the plan needs refining, rather than that there are no potential writers in your target area.

In 1999-2000, writernet, in partnership with Graeae and New Writing North, ran a mentoring scheme for disabled writers in the theatre. This description of their process of selection is quoted from the report on this scheme at www.writernet.co.uk. It seems exemplary in many ways and we offer it here as a valuable case study:

The fact that disabled writers write poetry and fiction much more readily than theatre pointed to a series of access issues. In consultation over many years with a range of disabled theatre practitioners, mentoring was identified as the most appropriate strategy for exploring and overcoming some of these.

Recruitment
The scheme was widely advertised in theatre and disability arts publications. Careful attention was given to accessing potential candidates. Mentees were selected for the scheme according to a process agreed by the steering panel.

Fifty writers applied to the scheme, with a shortlist of 12 interviewed before the final selection of seven was agreed.

Applications
The scheme was open to disabled writers at any level: beginners, those whose who had some experience and those who would consider themselves experienced. As a guide, the SHAPE (the national disability arts organisation) definition of disability was used:

People with physical, mental or sensory disabilities, with hidden disabilities, such as psoriasis, epilepsy, heart, chest conditions; people with disabilities linked to ageing; people suffering from mental illness.

Applicants were invited to submit between one and three ideas of less than 250 words, or a scene less than 10 pages double-spaced or lasting less than 10 minutes of stage time, and a CV and letter outlining what they hoped to achieve from the scheme. Sample ideas and information about the partner organisations were enclosed with details of the scheme for those interested in applying. Applications were welcomed in any format, including by email.

Interviews
Applicants were asked:
■ How would you aim to progress the ideas or sample scene that you submitted?

■ How do you think mentoring might work successfully for you?
■ What are your access needs and how might they be ideally met?
■ What kind of skills and experience would you look for in a mentor?
Do you have anyone in mind?
■ Where would you like your writing to be in three years' time?
■ Do you have anything you would like to ask us?

The steering panel used the interviews:
■ To clarify the nature of the scheme, its parameters, what was
expected of both mentors and mentees and the roles of writernet and
Graeae
■ To identify access needs and consider appropriate strategies to meet
them
■ To identify ways in which those needs might be met by a mentoring
relationship; and how the relationship might be best focused to enable
this to happen
■ To identify possible suitable mentors either from those who had
already put themselves forward, from the suggestions of those wishing
to be mentored, and from the panel's own knowledge
■ Finally, to make selections

This feels like a very well-thought-out and effective process for
identifying appropriate writers for a mentoring scheme. It is a model that
could be adapted to meet many situations.

It is perfectly possible to select mentees, as well as mentors, without
interviews, and this may sometimes be necessary, but it is desirable to
meet with all potential mentees if possible, because it makes the
'matching' of mentors and mentees much easier. (See above in the
section on how to select mentors.)
    If you are working with a more individual model of mentoring, like New
Writing North's, your process will obviously be less structured. (Some
ideas about how to identify writers who are well placed to profit from a
mentoring programme can be found in the chapter on mentees.) In
terms of identifying writers from specific groups, who are not coming to
you or your organisation, but whom you would like to serve, Jill Dawson
suggests asking experienced mentors from minority groups to put
forward applicants. An alternative might be to contact organisations
whose remit is within these communities and work in partnership with
them to identify suitable writers.

How do I match the two?

All the traditional wisdom insists that good matching is the key to successful mentoring. We have tried to address this from the point of view of both mentors and mentees in other chapters. Here is a summary of those ideas and some practical suggestions.

Mentoring works best when the mentor is genuinely excited by the *writing* (rather than sympathetic to the personality). All potential mentors should see a sample of the mentees' writing, and know something about their present development and their aims and ambitions. They should be given this opportunity under circumstances where they can refuse the work without personal embarrassment. The Writer's Pool sent mentors a selection of writing samples and asked them to choose their own mentees. New Writing North sends work from one writer to the prospective mentor in advance of any agreement to undertake a mentoring scheme.

Ideally, mentors and mentees should meet before they commit themselves, although this may not always be possible. Managers should hope at least that there will be some sort of personal friendship developing over the mentoring period and it is probably good to check that neither side has a strongly negative reaction to the other. Claire Malcolm, for example, always attends this meeting as a sort of marriage broker; and no one is committed until that meeting has taken place.

Several managers have found it useful to ask both sides directly whether there is someone they would like to work with. If the mentors are in place before the mentees, it can be a good idea to invite them into the selection process. If a mentee has a strong sense of an individual writer they would like for a mentor it can be worth pursuing this, at least as a possibility.

Individual circumstances need to be taken into account. On the writernet/Graeae scheme described above, some of the mentees had access or mobility problems that made it necessary that the mentoring took place in the mentee's home. For some mentors this might feel uncomfortable. Some writers enjoy online mentoring – others hate the very idea.

Mentors do not have to *be like* their mentees – by age, background, gender, writing style, non-writing interests or anything else. However in supporting writers from under-represented groups, the role model aspect of mentoring may be worth considering.

The better you know the widest possible pool of writers, and the more often you arrange mentoring partnerships, the more you will hone your matching skills.

There are after all no 'ideal' circumstances – and it is important not to be too precious about this. Good matching is felt to be key to good mentoring, but in fact distance learning schemes and even face-to-face ones have been successful where one or more of these conditions have not been possible. If both parties are enthusiastic about and understand the core values of mentoring this may be enough. We believe that people should not be excluded from mentoring because they are (for any good reason) unable to meet their mentor in advance.

How much might I be involved in the process?

In all manager-led mentoring projects the initial plan will have to be devised, developed and set up by you, including the selection – by whatever method – of the mentors and mentees. This initial phase may require involvement with the funders of the project.

We believe that both mentor and mentee should be offered contracts. In the Appendices, we have included a sample Mentoring Agreement. This is meant as a guide for individuals entering into their own contractual relationship, but does outline the areas that need to be addressed. A manager will obviously have some different priorities. The most obvious example will be that the contract is not between the mentor and the mentee, but between each of them separately and the managing organisation. This means, for example, that the idea that each mentoring session should be paid for at its opening is meaningless – or at least unnecessarily labyrinthine! A reasonable process might be to agree the overall payment and link the release of money to invoices and progress reports. New Writing North pays its mentors in three tranches – on signature, half-way through the agreed period, and at the end of the mentoring. The second two payments require not only an invoice but also a progress report. Some schemes require tight deadlines and specific amounts of time – these should be outlined in the contract and will need to be monitored. A New Writing North mentorship, in contrast, is a one-off and extremely flexible engagement. Frequency and type of meeting, size of submission and degree of contact is left up to the two writers. Either approach can work satisfactorily.

That mentors *should* be paid seems to us to be beyond question, although there are still people (nearly always managers or arts administrators!) who do not agree and argue that established writers will, or should, be happy to mentor for love alone. One important aspect of mentoring is to raise a writer's level of professionalism – this can hardly be 'taught' if mentors are expected to work for free. Furthermore, mentees should know what their mentors are being paid; this openness can enhance mentees' respect for the mentor, the process and themselves (knowing they are worth this to the manager) and allow them to complain without guilt if they are not getting a decent service.

How much mentors should be paid is presently an open question. New Writing North's approach enables partnerships to work out for themselves the balance of meeting time, reading time, travel time etc. But everyone involved needs to recognise that there is more work to mentoring than attending a two- or three-hour meeting every now and again. Creating, explaining and if necessary justifying the budget is clearly an important role for anyone managing mentoring.

Managers need to be involved in the practical aspects of setting up the relationship. On some schemes the best approach may be an induction day, where any difficulties can be addressed and where expectations can be established, in addition to bringing the participants together on neutral ground. Jan Rutherford, who runs a mentoring scheme for Scottish Book Trust, finds this approach not merely invaluable but also great fun. On smaller schemes it may be better simply to arrange a meeting between the two partners. (There is more about this in the section on training which follows.)

Managers also have the task of organising the end of the project – which will in many cases involve assessment and a written report. Both mentors and mentees should be required to submit a final report on their own experiences. In the case of a group scheme, it can be valuable to arrange a final 'event' of some sort, or set up ways in which participants can stay in touch with each other.

Other issues

Most mentoring in creative writing in the UK to date has been done 'experimentally'. There is no collected data on good practice, nor is it at all easy to locate and use the various assessment documents that individual organisations have put together describing their own practice and its relative merits. For example, there is a general sense that mentees do not need to be matched to their mentors by anything other than shared writing interests. However the (better recorded) information from the business sector, which has been using mentoring longer and more systematically, suggests that matching by both gender and race can have strong advantages. This may be particularly relevant when pursuing a social inclusion agenda. It is important at this juncture that we should try to accumulate more shared information on this topic, in order to prove the effectiveness of mentoring for writers.

However this in itself throws up a question about 'ownership', particularly in those mentoring relationships where there is a good deal of *written* exchange. In particular, issues of confidentiality and copyright need to be addressed. Does a mentor's response to a mentee's work belong to the mentor, to the management or to the mentee?

Could one properly use one's own letters or notes to writers one has mentored under a scheme paid for by a third party, as, for instance, part of a teaching course, or a book on mentoring of one's own? Can a manager ask a mentor for a report or reference on the abilities of a mentee?

For example, copyright turned out to be an important issue for participants on Crossing Borders. The British Council took a very clear line here – the 'creative writing' elements remained the 'property' of the mentees, but the commentaries, the mentors' supporting material and all other communication was copyright to the British Council. Crossing Borders moreover wanted to hold an archive for future research. This in turn created some difficulties around confidentiality, which in some situations (political or sexually explicit writing in some countries, for example) is a real and serious issue. The archive has removed names so that individual writers cannot be easily identified, but to be of any value, the commentaries need to be attached to the creative pieces, and therefore writers could potentially be identified in the future if a piece of writing was published.

Managers of mentoring schemes need to be at the very least aware of these issues and prepared to respond to them.

Maintenance

For most managers, the principal ongoing involvement with mentoring partnerships is troubleshooting, or mediating the relationship between mentor and mentee when this is not working smoothly. This seems to cause more anxiety than it need – because if you get the first bit right (making a careful selection of mentors and mentees and making sure there is a reasonable level of personal commitment on both sides before they start) there should not really be too many difficulties.

Sometimes what looks like a breakdown is in fact simply failed communication of the most practical kind: one or other of the partners has to go away, or gets ill, or more simply gets swallowed up in something else. It is obviously a good idea to set up a system so that you know if the two have not been communicating regularly (such as progress reports, a system of invoicing and occasional chats). Very often all that is needed is *information* and if the manager keeps in contact with both parties this ought to flow fairly smoothly.

However, no system is foolproof. As Jill Dawson puts it:

"The only thing that can go wrong is people. Breakdowns were due to personality clashes. The mentor who seeks an inappropriate personal relationship. The mentee who is too needy, presses the wrong buttons, does not respect the mentor's experience, or asks for awkward things."

Another cause of breakdown can be where there is an irreconcilable difference outside the writing relationship. Mentees can feel defensive if they do not know their assigned mentor's work, or wanted a different mentor. Everyone comes to the work with prejudices of their own. One thing that came up on Crossing Borders, for example, was religious faith. One mentee felt threatened and censored by the religion of her mentor, even though there did not seem to be much evidence that this was interfering with the work. No amount of interviewing or prior planning could have warned anyone of the problem – neither side was aware of it until it started to get in the way of the mentoring.

A different sort of problem comes up if the mentor cannot respect the mentee's work. Sometimes someone will present a very strong piece of writing as a submission, but it turns out that they simply do not have the ability or humility or energy to take it forward; or they are not able or willing to put in the amount of work and time that is required. This can be very frustrating for mentors, especially as they may not see forceful challenge as part of their role.

A different sort of problem arises where the expectations are not clear. Often mentees, despite everyone's best efforts, really do see mentoring as a way in to publishing and expect – or at least hope – that their mentor will introduce them to their own agent or editor. Mentors meanwhile are often anxiously and tenderly nurturing these relationships themselves and do not want to run any risks of that kind. In our model Agreement there is a clause specifically excluding the mentor from these sorts of obligations. This will not always be relevant – some mentoring is designed to develop precisely this phase of a writer's career – but it is important to think this through at the outset.

It is also surprisingly easy to focus exclusively on the mentee. Mentors, especially those without much experience, can easily feel insecure or undervalued and may need support.

An absolute necessity for successful mentoring is trust. If trust has been destroyed for whatever reason it is notoriously hard to re-establish. Obviously mediation is worth a try – especially if the problem arose from communications difficulties or misunderstanding at a practical level. But it may be easier and more effective in the long run to cut your losses: it may not be worth the effort to endlessly try to repair fractured relationships, since without a sturdy relationship the whole project will probably not deliver much in the longer term.

"If the relationship breaks down, diplomacy by the manager to make it right takes a lot of effort and is unlikely to succeed. The quickest thing is to find alternatives. If that's not possible and there's no way round it,

then the mentee loses the place and the mentor loses the money. That potential loss gives the participants an incentive to work things through."
Jill Dawson

Because breakdowns do happen, although not as often as might be expected, it is important that the contract specifies what will happen in such circumstances. The Writers' Pool, in the quotation above, took the position that the mentor would lose the remaining part of the fee; on Crossing Borders – partly because many of the African mentees had lives of great complexity and difficulty – the mentors were paid for the whole project even if their mentees were not able to complete the programme for any reason (except mentor negligence). The important thing here is that the process, whatever you choose, should be clear from the outset.

Overall, the degree of involvement on the part of managers tends to vary considerably, according to the nature of the particular mentoring scheme. It is the manager's role to support both the mentee and the mentor through the experience and to be a sounding board throughout. In an ideal world you set up the partnerships and they get on with it, sending you an occasional progress report and a great deal of thanks for such a happy and useful professional development opportunity!

What sort of training should I offer mentors?

There is presently no recognised training or qualification for mentors of creative writing. There is no quality assurance and no national resource for locating experienced mentors, or which new or would-be mentors can approach looking for work. Yet experience suggests that whenever a project advertises for mentors there is an enormous amount of interest in the work.

If you are involved with a group of new or inexperienced mentors, it may well be worth running an induction day – either for mentors and mentees together, or for the mentors alone. A number of other larger schemes, including The Writers' Pool, the Scottish Book Trust (mentors and mentees) and Crossing Borders (mentors only) have used induction days. Such days have been specific to the project and open only to those already selected, rather than generic training, as a means of qualifying to become a mentor.

This is interesting because there is in fact an extensive network of training programmes for mentors in other fields, not just corporate enterprises, but within the voluntary, educational and public service sectors – including academic writing.

At one level, this probably may not matter very much at the moment. The quantity of mentoring that is going on, mainly under the supervision of stable arts development organisations, can probably work most efficiently and economically without a new administrative tier. On the base line, good mentoring is a personal skill, not a professional one, and managers are experienced in selection procedures and follow-up support, and everything in the garden is rosy. Certainly, personal knowledge of a potential mentor is probably as valuable as yet another certificate announcing a 'qualification'.

However, there are issues that are beginning to emerge that need some thought. There is no clear, shared concept about what mentoring is or how a mentor should proceed. Even if a writer has been a mentor before, this does not necessarily mean they expect to deliver the same sort of 'product' as the next mentor. Even cursory training would provide a point of departure for a discussion about how an individual mentor likes to work.

The question of access to mentoring applies to mentors as well as to mentees. Mentoring is good professional work, which many writers enjoy doing and which certainly enhances their CVs and their incomes. The dangers of cliques, and the consequent exclusion of people not in the loop, is a chronic problem within arts funding. Unless you have a very tight geographical remit and a very strong writers' infrastructure it is highly possible that you are not in contact with potentially excellent mentors, or that their names do not come to mind. Some sort of training might at the very least provide opportunities to *meet* writers who are expressing real interest in mentoring.

Mentoring is a growth area. Quite apart from targeted schemes and larger projects there is an increasing desire among writers to work with a mentor. As we have seen, Arts Council England is now able to fund mentoring through its Grants for the Arts scheme, and commercial mentoring, both through organisations and as an individually offered service, appears to be burgeoning. Writers who wish to employ a mentor may know a particular writer they want to work with and be confident enough to set up and manage such a relationship. But often the very writers who would gain most from mentoring are those without that sort of contact. Increasingly, literary development agencies, as well as individual writers, are going to be approached for recommendations and suggestions as to how to find a mentor. Some sort of training would allow would-be mentors to find out more, to discover whether this way of working is something they would like to be engaged in, and to have some external validation of their seriousness, without committing themselves to a newer writer and a possibly fragile relationship.

No sort of training is going to stop individuals forming partnerships, friendships and co-mentoring arrangements; nor would anyone want this to happen. None the less there is a responsibility on managers and some sort of short training would relieve them of this burden.

However, a shortage of trained mentors should not discourage people from venturing into this arena. Writers, both as mentors and mentees, like mentoring and derive benefits from mentoring, at a wide range of points in their careers. It would appear to be cost effective and a valuable tool for professional development.

Appendices

As well as a list of useful contacts, this section also contains a number of model agreements which can be used as starting points for drawing up your own contracts. These documents are also available as Word files to download from www.newwritingnorth.com/careers/careers.php.

Appendix one

SAMPLE MENTORING AGREEMENT

This agreement is between:

_____   Mentee

and

_____   Mentor

1. AIM OF THE PROJECT
In this section, the manager needs to agree the goals and wider aims of the project (which might be: work editorially to create a collection of poetry, work on the structure of a novel in progress, develop a series of short stories etc).

The sessions will concentrate on developing the mentee's writing skills. The mentor is not expected to promote the mentee's writing or specifically help to find avenues of publication during the mentoring process.

2. DELIVERY PROCESS
The mentor and mentee will agree and write down the mentee's goals at the first meeting. These goals will be reviewed at each meeting and will form the basis for the evaluation of the project at the end of the contract.

The mentee will provide written materials for that meeting at least one week in advance. The mentor will have studied those materials in advance of each session. The mentee will provide any necessary notes that might assist the mentor in appreciating the material and preparing appropriately for the session.

After each meeting the mentor will write to the mentee and summarise the main points of the meeting. A copy of this letter should be sent to [the managing agency].

3. CONFIDENTIALITY & COPYRIGHT OF MATERIALS
The mentor will treat the mentee's writing in full confidence and not share that work with anyone else. The mentor owns copyright to any of the mentor's own writings delivered as part of the scheme.

4. IN THE EVENT OF A BREAKDOWN IN THE RELATIONSHIP

Should the mentoring relationship break down in any way, and no third party be able to repair it, the mentoring relationship will stop and nothing more be due from either party except for the full payment of fees up to the point of breakdown. Breakdown is constituted by either party refusing to continue.

5. THE ROLE OF THE MANAGER

The role of [the managing agency] as the programme manager in this relationship is to help to create goals for the project, issue contracts to mentor and mentee, monitor and evaluate the process by keeping in contact with both parties during the duration of the project and by supporting the relationship on both sides. Before a relationship breaks down, [the managing agency] should be the first port of call for both mentor and mentee.

6. EVALUATION

[The managing agency] as the funding body is also responsible for reporting to funders on the project and as such may require participants to engage in both written and verbal evaluation with [the managing agency] or other third party evaluators.

Mentor's evaluation report

The report should include a summary of the following:
- The goals that were set at the beginning of the project.
- The process of mentoring and how the mentee responded to the process.
- An appraisal of the highlights and difficulties of the project and explanations if relevant.
- Things that could have been done differently or better to enhance the process.
- A statement on how far you think that the mentee has come via the process.
- Your appraisal of how [the managing agency] managed the scheme from your perspective.

Mentee's evaluation report

The report should include a summary of the following:
- A review of the goals that were set at the beginning of the project and an appraisal of whether you feel that you have met them.
- What it was like to work with your mentor over the period of the scheme.
- The highlights and low points of the project and explanations if relevant.

■ Anything that you feel that you could have done differently to benefit more from the experience.
■ A general statement on the value of the experience to you.
■ Your appraisal of how [the managing agency] managed the scheme from your perspective.

7. TIMESCALE

The mentor agrees to provide creative mentoring, on a one-to-one basis, for a period of _____.

Over that period the mentor and mentee will meet on ___ occasions. These meetings will take place at intervals of no longer than ___ weeks. Dates and venues are as mutually agreed. Communications between mentor and mentee will be restricted to the times of submission of materials and the actual mentoring sessions, unless a matter of emergency.

8. RESCHEDULING OF MEETINGS

Should either party need to reschedule a session, at least 48 hours notice should be given and a mutually convenient alternative date agreed. Should the mentor and not the mentee attend a session, that session will be deemed to have been delivered and must be paid for.

9. EQUALITY

Both parties must adhere and respect [the managing agency's] Equality Mission Statement which forms part of this contract for services. Should either party act in any way which compromises this statement during the duration of this contract, [the managing agency] reserves the right to end the contract and if necessary to seek repayment of any fees which have been paid in advance.

10. PAYMENTS TO THE MENTOR

Payment to the mentor will be at the rate of £___ per session, including preparation and travel time. The total fee payable for this contract of work is £___.

Here you need to specify the payment schedule.

Payment will be made in two instalments: 75% at the beginning of the contract and the second payment of 25% on receipt of the evaluation report on the project. The report must be received no later than ____. Late delivery of the project report may result in the non-payment of the final invoice.

Payments will be released following the receipt of invoices from the mentor. This contract is made on a freelance basis and [the managing agency] is not liable to cover the costs of National Insurance in relation to the fees for work.

I agree to abide by this contract: *(NB copies of the contract to be signed and given to each participating party.)*

SIGNED: Mentee   Date

SIGNED: Mentor   Date

SIGNED: Manager   Date

Appendix two

MENTOR'S EVALUATION REPORT

Name:
Address:

Phone:
Email:

Name of mentee:

From: To:

1. Please outline the goals that were set at the beginning of the scheme.

2. To what extent do you feel these goals have been met/not met?

3. What was it like to work with your mentee over the period of the scheme?

4. How did they respond to being mentored?

5. What were the high and low points of the project?

6. From your perspective, how well was the scheme managed by [the managing agency]?

7. Is there anything that you think could have been done differently or better to enhance the process?

8. Do you think the scheme offered value for money?

9. Any other comments?

Signed: Date:

Appendix three

MENTEE'S EVALUATION REPORT

Name:
Address:

Phone:
Email:

Name of mentor:

From: To:

1. Please outline the goals that were set at the beginning of the scheme.

2. To what extent do you feel these goals have been met/not met?

3. What was it like to work with your mentor over the period of the scheme?

4. What were the high and low points of the project?

5. Is there anything that you feel could have been done differently by [the managing agency] to support you in benefiting more from the experience?

6. Is there anything you personally would do differently if you were to start the scheme again?

7. Please provide a general statement on the value of this scheme to your career.

8. Any other comments?

Signed: Date:

Appendix four

FUNDING YOUR MENTORING SCHEME

1. National arts councils

Arts Council England
The national development agency for the arts in England. Funding for the professional development of writers is available through the Grants for the Arts programme. There is extensive information about applying to Grants for the Arts in the funding section on the Arts Council England website. A good place to start is the Frequently Asked Questions document. It's also worth checking with your regional Arts Council England office to see when they are next holding a Grants for the Arts seminar for potential applicants. An individual advice session may also be available. In any case, it is important to make contact with your regional literature/theatre officer before applying.
www.artscouncil.org.uk

The Arts Council of Northern Ireland
The lead development agency for the arts in Northern Ireland. Funding for writers is available through the Support for the Individual Artist Programme. **www.artscouncil-ni.org**

Scottish Arts Council
The lead body for the funding, development and advocacy of the arts in Scotland. Writers can apply to the Professional Development Fund for funding for mentoring. **www.scottisharts.org.uk**

Writers based in the Highlands and Islands of Scotland can apply to the HI~Arts Writers' Professional Development Scheme for support with mentoring costs. Further details on the HI~Arts website.
www.hi-arts.co.uk

In Wales, writers interested in mentoring should contact Academi, the Welsh National Literature Promotion Agency and Society for Writers, which runs a mentoring service for writers, aimed at writers in whose work publishers have already expressed a firm interest. Further details on the Academi website at **www.academi.org**. Funding for mentoring isn't available from The Arts Council of Wales.

2. Support organisations for the creative and cultural sector

There are a large number of national and regional organisations in the UK dedicated to supporting professional development in the creative and cultural sector. They are a good source of information and advice on sources of funding and some can also provide funding directly. For example, Northern Cultural Skills (**www.ncsp.co.uk**) can provide financial support towards the costs of mentoring for those living and working in the north east of England, while in Cornwall, Creative Skills (**www.creativeskills.org.uk**) operates a development fund, which can be used to part-fund a wide range of professional development activity including mentoring. CreativePeople (**www.creativepeople.org.uk**) is a national network of over 100 of these organisations and is a good starting point.

Another good source of information and advice on potential sources of funding is the nationwide Business Link service, which maintains a comprehensive grants and support directory. For details of your nearest Business Link, contact 0845 600 9006 (minicom 0845 606 2666) or visit the Business Link website (**www.businesslink.org**). Operating alongside Business Link is a growing network of creative and cultural industries development agencies – organisations that provide specialist business support for the creative and cultural sector. Your local Business Link will have details.

3. Charitable trusts and foundations

FunderFinder (**www.funderfinder.org.uk**) produces an easy to use software programme called People in Need that can help you to identify charitable trusts and foundations that provide grants to individuals for education (in the broadest sense – including professional development). It's widely available (often held in local libraries) and free to use. Some regional Arts Council England offices provide this service. Contact FunderFinder on 0113 243 3008 for your nearest access point.

Other useful sources of information on charitable funding include *The Educational Grants Directory*, *The Directory of Grant-making Trusts*, *A Guide to the Major Trusts*, *A Guide to Scottish Trusts* and *The Welsh Funding Guide*. All are published by the Directory of Social Change (**www.dsc.org.uk**) and copies are available in most public reference libraries.

4. Useful sources of information

The literaturetraining website (**www.literaturetraining.com**) has regularly updated information on sources of funding for professional development in its funding section and there's an information sheet with useful tips on applying for funding. It's also worth checking the listing of bursaries, fellowships and grants in *The Writer's Handbook* and of prizes and awards in *The Writers' and Artists' Yearbook* for any that might support the costs of mentoring.

Other key sources of information and advice on possible sources of funding for mentoring, especially those that might be available regionally, are literature development officers and literature or writing development organisations. The literature or theatre officer at your national arts council or Arts Council England regional office (an important source of information and advice in their own right) will be able to give you contact details for those in your area or you can visit the National Association for Literature Development website (**www.nald.org**). It's also worth contacting your local authority arts development officer.

Appendix five

USEFUL CONTACTS

Funding agencies

Arts Council England
14 Great Peter Street
London SW1P 3NQ
Tel: 0845 300 6200
Email: enquiries@artscouncil.org.uk
Web: www.artscouncil.org.uk

The Scottish Arts Council
12 Manor Place
Edinburgh EH3 7DD
Tel: 0131 226 6051
Email: help.desk@scottisharts.org.uk
Web: www.scottisharts.org.uk

The Arts Council of Northern Ireland
77 Malone Road
Belfast BT9 6AQ
Tel: 28 9035 8200
Email: info@artscouncil-ni.org
Web: www.artscouncil-ni.org

The British Council
10 Spring Gardens
London SW1A 2BN
Tel: 020 7930 8466
Email: general.enquiries@britishcouncil.org
Web: www.britishcouncil.org

Literature development agencies

New Writing North
Culture Lab
Newcastle University
King's Walk
Newcastle upon Tyne NE1 7RU
Tel: 0191 222 1332
Email: mail@newwritingnorth.com
Web: www.newwritingnorth.com

Academi
3rd floor
Mount Stuart House
Mount Stuart Square
Cardiff CF10 5FQ
Tel: 029 2047 2266
Email: post@academi.org
Web: www.academi.org

National Association of Writers in Education
PO Box 1
Sheriff Hutton
York YO60 7YU
Tel: 01653 618429
Email: paul@nawe.org.uk
Web: www.nawe.co.uk

New Writing South
9 Jew Street
Brighton
East Sussex BN1 1UT
Tel: 01273 735353
Web: www.newwritingsouth.com

The New Writing Partnership
4-6 Netherconesford
93-95 King Street
Norwich NR1 1PW
Tel: 01603 877177
Email: info@newwritingpartnership.org.uk
Web: www.newwritingpartnership.org.uk

HI~Arts
Ballantyne House
84 Academy Street
Inverness
IV1 1LU Scotland
Tel: 01463 717 091
Email : info@hi-arts.co.uk
Web: www.hi-arts.co.uk

Booktrust
Book House
45 East Hill
London SW18 2QZ
Tel: 020 8516 2977
Email: query@booktrust.org.uk
Web: www.booktrust.org.uk

Scottish Booktrust
Sandeman House
Trunk's Close
55 High Street
Edinburgh EH1 1SR
Tel: 0131 524 0160
Email: info@scottishbooktrust.com
Web: www.scottishbooktrust.com

The National Association for Literature Development
PO Box 49657
London N8 7YZ
Tel: 020 7272 8386
Email: director@nald.org
Web: www.nald.org

Literature Training
PO BOX 23595
Edinburgh EH6 7YX
Tel: 0131 553 2210
Email: info@literaturetraining.com
Web: www.literaturetraining.com

The Arvon Foundation
42a Buckingham Palace Road
London SW1W 0RE
Tel: 020 7931 7611
Email: London@arvonfoundation.org
Web: www.arvonfoundation.org

Spread the Word
77 Lambeth Walk
London SE11 6DX
Tel: 020 7735 3111
Email: info@spreadtheword.org.uk
Web: www.spreadtheword.org.uk

Others

The Society of Authors
84 Drayton Gardens
London SW10 9SB
Tel: 020 7373 6642
Web: www.societyofauthors.net

The Literary Consultancy
Diorama Arts
No 1 Euston Centre
London NW1 3JG
Tel: 020 7813 4330
Email: info@literaryconsultancy.co.uk
Web: www.literaryconsultancy.co.uk

Writernet
Cabin V
Clarendon Buildings
25 Horsell Road
London N5 1XL
Tel: 020 7609 7474
Email: info@writernet.co.uk
Web: www.writernet.co.uk

ABOUT THE AUTHORS

Sara Maitland is an award-winning novelist who also writes in a wide variety of other genres, including non-fiction, radio drama and short stories. Her most recent book is a collection of stories, *On Becoming a Fairy Godmother* (Maia). She has worked as a mentor for New Writing North and other organisations. She was the mentor co-ordinator for Crossing Borders, a joint project of the British Council and Lancaster University, which delivered mentoring to over 300 emerging African writers. She is currently writing a book about silence.

Martin Goodman has a PhD in creative writing, lectures on English and creative writing at Plymouth University, and has mentored many professional and emerging writers in America, Britain and Africa. He is an award-winning writer of novels, biography, travel literature, short stories and plays. His latest book is *Suffer and Survive*, a biography of the scientist Dr JS Haldane (Simon & Schuster, 2007). His most recent novel is *Slippery When Wet* (Transita, 2006). For more information, see www.martingoodman.com.